Redefining the
Comprehensive Experience

Bedford Way Papers

ISSN 0261—0078

Redefining the Comprehensive Experience

Clyde Chitty (editor), Carol Adams, Bernard Barker,
Michael Fielding, Margaret Maden and Michael Young

Introduction by Denis Lawton

Bedford Way Papers 32
INSTITUTE OF EDUCATION
University of London

First published in 1987 by the Institute of Education, University of London,
20 Bedford Way, London WC1H 0AL.

Distributed by Turnaround Distribution Ltd., 27 Horsell Road,
London N5 1XL (telephone: 01-609 7836).

The opinions expressed in these papers are those of the authors and do not necessarily
reflect those of the publisher.

British Library Cataloguing in Publication Data

Redefining the comprehensive experience. — (Bedford Way papers, ISSN 0261-0078; 32).
  1. Education, Secondary — England
  1. Comprehensive high schools — England
  2. Chitty, Clyde   II. Series.
  373.2'5'0942   LA635

ISBN 0-85473-280-2

Typeset by Acies Print Ltd, Leicester
Printed in Great Britain by Billing & Sons Ltd, Worcester and London

The Welfare and Felicity therefore of every State and Kingdom require that the Knowledge of the Working Poor should be confined within the Verge of their Occupations, and never extended (as to things visible) beyond what relates to their Calling.

Bernard Mandeville, *The Fable of the Bees,* 1714.

My plan of instruction is extremely simple and limited. They learn, on weekdays, such coarse works as may fit them for servants. I allow of no writing for the poor. My object is not to make them fanatics, but to train up the lower classes in habits of industry and piety.

R. Brimley Johnson (ed.), *The Letters of Hannah More,* (c.1790). The Bodley Head, 1925.

★　　★　　★

The kind of education in which I am interested is not one which will adapt workers to the existing industrial regime; I am not sufficiently in love with the regime for that. It seems to me that the business of all those who would not be educational time-servers is to resist every move in this direction, and to strive for a kind of vocational education which will first alter the existing industrial system, and ultimately transform it.

John Dewey, *The New Republic,* 5 May 1915.

Far too many boys and girls . . . are still being allowed to write themselves off well below their true potential.

Lord Boyle of Handsworth in an Afterword to School of Barbiana, *Letter to a Teacher.* Penguin, 1970.

Contents

Acknowledgements

I should like to thank Maurice Holt, Denis Lawton, Carrie Maynard, Brian Simon, Jim Thawley, John White and Michael Young for all their help and advice in the preparation of this Paper. Above all I owe a special debt of gratitude to Denis Baylis, who has played such an active and supportive role in this venture from the very beginning.

C. C.

Notes on Contributors

Carol Adams is inspector for equal opportunities with the Inner London Education Authority. She has researched and written on the issue of equal opportunities for the past fifteen years, and has published and edited a number of books for school students on gender issues and women's history.

Bernard Barker was educated at one of the earliest and largest London comprehensives (Eltham Green), graduating to become head of Stanground School, Peterborough, in 1980. He is current chair of the Cambridgeshire Association of Secondary Heads. His publications include *Rescuing the Comprehensive Experience* (Open University, 1986), the 'History Replay' series for Blackwell, Longman History Games and studies for the *International Review of Social History* and *History Workshop*.

Clyde Chitty (editor) has spent twenty years teaching in comprehensive schools in London and Leicestershire. He is now a lecturer in the Curriculum Studies Department at the Institute of Education, University of London. He is the author of numerous articles on the history and politics of education, and has written and presented a number of programmes for radio and television. He was a founder member of the Comprehensive Schools Committee in 1965 and has been on the editorial board of *Forum* since 1974.

Michael Fielding is a deputy head at Stantonbury Campus, Milton Keynes. He has taught in comprehensive schools for the past eighteen years and has published mainly in the field of applied philosophy. Particular areas of interest to him are democracy in education; pursuit of the positive alternative to a competitive, hierarchical model of schooling; the critique of managerialism; and a communitarian paradigm for the comprehensive school.

Denis Lawton is director of the Institute of Education, University of London, where he was previously professor of curriculum studies. He has made a particular study of the control of the school curriculum. His previous publications include *The Politics of the School Curriculum* (Routledge and Kegan Paul, 1980), *Curriculum Studies and Educational Planning* (Hodder and Stoughton, 1983) and, most recently (with Peter Gordon), *HMI* (Routledge and Kegan Paul, 1987).

Margaret Maden is principal adviser for tertiary planning and development for the Inner London Education Authority. She was director of the Islington Sixth-Form Centre for three years, and previously headmistress of Islington Green Comprehensive School. She has been involved in the continuing public debate on comprehensive and continuing education through journal articles and contributions to radio and television discussions. In October 1987 she takes up the post of deputy chief education officer for Warwickshire.

Michael Young is senior lecturer in sociology of education and co-ordinator of the Post-Sixteen Education Centre at the Institute of Education, University of London. He has published widely on sociological aspects of the secondary curriculum. His current research interests are in the problems of introducing technology across the curriculum, and the development of a vocationally-based model of general education.

Abbreviations Used

APU	Assessment of Performance Unit
B/TEC	Business and Technician Education Council
CBI	Confederation of British Industry
CEA	Conservative Education Association
CGLI	City and Guilds of London Institute
CPVE	Certificate of Pre-Vocational Education
CSE	Certificate of Secondary Education
CTC	City Technology College
CVCP	Committee of Vice-Chancellors and Principals
DES	Department of Education and Science
DofE	Department of Employment
FEU	Further Education Unit
GCE	General Certificate of Education
GCSE	General Certificate of Secondary Education
GRIST	Grant Related In-Service Training
HMI	Her Majesty's Inspectorate
ILEA	Inner London Education Authority
LAPP	Lower Attaining Pupils Programme
LEA	Local Education Authority
MAP	Manchester Assessment Project
MSC	Manpower Services Commission
NAFE	Non-Advanced Further Education
NAHT	National Association of Head Teachers
NCVQ	National Council for Vocational Qualifications
NEDC	National Economic Development Council
NUT	National Union of Teachers
OCEA	Oxford Certificate of Educational Achievement
SEG	Southern Examining Group
TRIST	TVEI Related In-Service Training
TUC	Trades Union Congress
TVEI	Technical and Vocational Education Initiative
YOP	Youth Opportunities Programme
YTS	Youth Training Scheme

Introduction

Denis Lawton

All the contributors to this study are strong supporters of comprehensive education. They are responding to two sets of issues: first, criticisms of the idea (or ideal) of comprehensive schooling which started in a serious way in 1969 (with the publication of the first of the Black Papers) and have had a renewed lease of life in the last ten years when comprehensive schools have been singled out for attacks in the media by politicians on the Right, and by a number of theorists writing about education. Second, there is the need to redefine the aims of comprehensive education in the light of social, economic, political and educational changes which have taken place since the 1960s.

Either of these two tasks would have been difficult to treat adequately in one slim volume, and it may seem bold to attempt to accomplish both at the same time. But, in some respects, they are both aspects of the same problem, and it has seemed better to try to tackle a whole range of contemporary issues, even if it will not prove possible to deal with any one of them exhaustively. We can be sure that this will not be the last book looking at these issues.

Each of the contributors has addressed the problem in a different way. Clyde Chitty, as editor, has made no attempt to impose a rigid formula. In that sense it may be better to see this book as a collection of essays about comprehensive education rather than as a single sustained linear argument.

The main critics of comprehensive education fall into two very rough categories. On the one hand there are those who attack the comprehensive ideal from the point of view of empirical studies. Beverley Shaw, for example, has examined schools and then gone on to question some of the fundamental ideas behind comprehensive education. On the other hand there are those like Roger Scruton, whose attacks are on the ideas themselves without the necessity of gathering evidence. But very often the lack of evidence does not prevent judgements of a practical nature which rest on assumed evidence to support the argument. To address each of those criticisms in detail would have needed a very different book. Maybe such a book is desirable and necessary, but this volume refers only in passing to the ideological and philosophical standpoint of the Right.

Then there are various changes that have affected the developing schools — social, economic, political and, not least, educational changes. The social changes would include, for example, the fact that since the 1960s the United Kingdom has become much more a multicultural society. This fact should, of course, influence the curriculum of *all* comprehensive schools, and it is a pity that concerns about multicultural education usually crop up only in those inner-city areas where other problems exist and confuse the issue. But clearly the task of all comprehensive schools now in terms of educating for a multicultural society is very different from the situation in the late 1940s or early 1950s. Similarly, the issue of equality of opportunities from a gender point of view is much more salient now than it was twenty years or more ago. Some writers have assumed that comprehensive schools would be mixed in terms of gender (as well as class and ability); others have assumed that one of the tasks of a comprehensive school would be to ensure that kind of equality of opportunity. But the issues now are concerned with detailed matters of curriculum planning, rather than simple ideals. Many schools have done extremely well in adjusting to these changes. But some of the most bitter critics of comprehensive schools have attacked teachers for indulging in 'social engineering' rather than reform of education.

The economic changes to which comprehensive schools have had to adjust include the rapidly rising rate of unemployment of young people. One of the ironies of the present situation is that at the very time when the link between schooling and employment is weakening very dramatically, schools have been urged to make the curriculum much more relevant to the needs of 'the world of work'. And this constitutes an added complication to the problem of school organization in a variety of ways. Clyde Chitty shows how this has been a prominent feature of the education debate since the Ruskin College Speech of 1976.

Political changes have also affected the schools directly and indirectly. Although Clyde Chitty is obviously correct in pointing out that 1979 does not represent the date when all policies suddenly changed in education, it is nevertheless true that 1979 (or possibly February, 1975, when Margaret Thatcher succeeded Edward Heath as leader of the Conservative Party) represents the emergence of the New Right politically and the beginning of a threat to consensus over a number of welfare and social issues, including education. This new lack of consensus on such questions as comprehensive education has not only licensed even more vigorous attacks on comprehensive schools in the media and elsewhere; it has also led to a serious undermining of the comprehensive system itself.

Various contributors to this book will give examples of the Conservative Government's policies which have not only weakened the state system of education generally, but have, in particular, cast doubt on comprehensive schools as the normal secondary route. And, of course, private schools continue to flourish, and have, in fact, been given a new lease of life by the introduction of the Assisted Places Scheme in September, 1981.

Finally, education, both theory and practice, has not stood still in the last twenty or thirty years. Changes in curriculum and pedagogy have been advocated and have been put into practice in many comprehensive schools. Most of them involve greater demands on teachers and a heightening of their professional skills. No one pretends that all the problems of comprehensive schools have been solved — there is still, for example, a problem of under-achievement in many schools. But perhaps the unfairest kind of criticism has been to attack comprehensive schools, citing as examples some inner-city schools, for failing to solve problems which are as much social as they are educational. No educational system can put right such social evils as bad housing, poverty and inadequate services.

*   *   *

All the contributors address some of these problems in different ways, mostly from their own direct experience of comprehensive education.

Clyde Chitty, who has had many years' experience of teaching in London comprehensive schools, as well as being Vice-Principal and Acting Principal of Earl Shilton Community College in Leicestershire, addresses three aspects of the problem in his first chapter. Why is it that comprehensive schools have been so unfairly attacked? In what ways are they changing? What are the particular events, especially since 1976, which are connected with these changes? His analysis is perceptive and challenging.

Michael Young, Co-ordinator for the Post-16 Education Centre at the University of London Institute of Education, takes up one of the themes outlined by his colleague, Clyde Chitty, and develops it in much greater detail: the issue of vocationalization. He is sceptical of some of the moves in the direction of vocational education, whilst recognizing that some kind of departure from the over-academic curriculum was desirable and necessary. He is critical of the way that changes have been forced on schools and colleges

— incidentally making the task of some of them even more difficult. At the same time, he believes that contradictions within current policy may become sources of political change based upon new demands and new social movements.

Bernard Barker, Headteacher of Stanground School in Cambridgeshire and the first comprehensive headteacher to have been educated in a comprehensive school, examines some of the aspects of the history of comprehensive development and cautions us against a 'retreat to basics' or a return to the traditional grammar school curriculum. At the same time he takes issue with progressive and vocational approaches because neither really believes in education for its own sake. Most educational experiences are, he argues, justifiable in their own right, not as 'exercises in a phrenological gymnasium'.

Michael Fielding, of Stantonbury Campus, Milton Keynes, is also seeking a paradigm. Some of his suggestions have much in common with the approach adopted by David Hargreaves in *The Challenge for the Comprehensive School* (1982). Fraternity is a key word in his approach. He also spells out the move from 'equality of opportunity' to 'equal value' as a principle behind comprehensive education. He draws upon some of his earlier experiences in Thomas Bennett Community College in Crawley, in support of this view. He also has some interesting points to make about the comprehensive school curriculum, based on the experience of Stantonbury Campus. There is much in this contribution to give encouragement to teachers in schools where, perhaps, they have not yet quite reached the stage of curriculum planning which is possible at Stantonbury.

Carol Adams, of the Inner London Education Authority, addresses the three problems of gender, race and class, which she suggests are 'essential issues for comprehensive education'. It is perhaps symptomatic of the existing political situation that some of the most bitter attacks on comprehensive schools have been associated with those attempting to introduce these equality of opportunity issues into the school curriculum. Carol Adams associates this curriculum development process with the need to 'demystify the curriculum'. But it is not, of course, simply a matter of the curriculum: it is a question of the ethos of the whole school.

Margaret Maden draws upon her experience as Director of Islington Sixth Form Centre to talk about the particular issue of 16-19 education. She attacks the notion of education for the few, and a narrow skilled-based training for the many. In effect she is arguing for a continuation of the comprehensive school idea up to the age of nineteen and beyond. A major development here is that students of this age group must be treated as young adults. The world of work is certainly not irrelevant in this context, but it is only one aspect of adult life. Education must be concerned with much more than narrow training. To end at that point might have placed too great an emphasis on the defects of the present system. Clyde Chitty has, however, provided a useful and constructive conclusion pointing the way ahead. He argues that teachers have to find ways of utilizing and exploiting current initiatives to serve democratic and progressive ends. There is no point in simply waiting for political changes that may or may not happen. It is a suitably positive message of hope for the future, based on the reality of the present.

The Comprehensive Principle Under Threat

Clyde Chitty

It is commonly alleged in the national press and on radio and television that there is something seriously wrong with our state education system. The term 'crisis' is widely used in outbursts, amounting at times to hysteria, which are strongly reminiscent of some of the wilder statements of the early Black Papers. When, for example, *The Comprehensive Experiment* (Reynolds, Sullivan and Murgatroyd) was published at the end of April 1987, showing how, from the authors' idiosyncratic standpoint, the reform movement had gone astray, it was immediately seized upon as a convenient weapon in the pre-election campaign against comprehensive schools. Former Bradford headteacher Ray Honeyford used it in a full-page article in the *Daily Mail* (1 May) to argue that the comprehensive system had failed; and Stuart Sexton, former special adviser to Sir Keith Joseph, wrote to the *Independent* (4 May) proclaiming with enthusiasm that selection should be reintroduced.

It could be argued that Conservative Government ministers have, in fact, played a major role in both creating and exploiting this 'crisis' mentality. And the most convenient targets for their denigration have been our comprehensive schools and the teachers who staff them. Interviewed by Matthew Parris on ITV's *Weekend World* programme at the beginning of December 1986, the Education Secretary Kenneth Baker talked in terms of the present system being 'seriously flawed'. In his view, the great hopes of those early believers that 'comprehensive schools were going to solve everything' had been cruelly dashed — which was 'a great pity'. Such sentiments have become the justification for a whole series of radical proposals which point to the reintroduction of selection. Indeed, Margaret Thatcher told the Young Conservatives Conference at Scarborough in February 1987 that the abolition of the grammar schools was 'one of the biggest mistakes ever made' (quoted in the *Guardian*, 9 February 1987). And in a pre-election interview with the editor of the *Daily Mail* she said:

'We are going much further with education than we ever thought of doing before.' Going further would include the reversing of 'this universal comprehensives thing'. As Minister for Education in the Heath Government she had found it 'difficult if not impossible to stop . . . this great rollercoaster of an idea'. But now she looked forward to 'the breaking-up of the giant comprehensives' (*Daily Mail*, 13 May 1987).

What is the background to the present situation; and why is the Thatcher Government so determined to dismantle the system of comprehensive schools or, at the very least, to transform it once again into a system of selective or differentiated schools? Can it justifiably be claimed that the comprehensive schools have failed the pupils and parents of this country? This introductory chapter looks at the history of the comprehensive reform since 1960 and, in particular, at the trends and developments of the last ten years as they affect the eleven-to-sixteen age range. Later chapters, and particularly those of Michael Young and Margaret Maden, look at the problem of providing a comprehensive experience for the sixteen-to-nineteen group.

The history of the comprehensive reform, 1960-76

According to recent official statistics (*Social Trends 16*, 1986, p.205), more than 90 per cent of local authority pupils now attend non-selective schools in England (more in Wales and nearly 100 per cent in Scotland). Yet, as Gregory has pointed out (*The Times Educational Supplement*, 6 February 1987):

> Twenty years of officially recognized comprehensive education have failed to produce strong definitive statements about the criteria and values upon which the genuinely comprehensive school should be based. HMI reports do not include any attempt to evaluate the extent to which a secondary school may be genuinely comprehensive. This makes it difficult to reply to those whose constant preoccupation is the perpetuation of myths about the alleged lack of competence of our comprehensive schools.

Current confusion about the aims and objectives of education in general and of comprehensive schools in particular has arisen at a time of contraction and doubt. As Bernbaum has observed (Bernbaum, 1979, pp.1-2): 'essentially, the educational story of the last few years is one of a retreat from optimism and a decline not only in the value placed upon education but also in the scale of the enterprise'. And this retreat and decline can be understood only in the light of the dreams and aspirations which characterized those who campaigned for change in the 1960s.

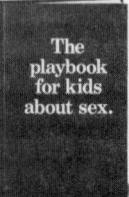

'We are going much further with education than we ever thought of doing before.' Margaret Thatcher, interviewed in the *Daily Mail*, 13 May 1987. A selection of 1987 general election publicity which illustrates how education was a prime campaign issue.

At a time of expansion and optimism, it was widely believed that the educational system could be changed in such a way as to produce greater equality, social justice and economic efficiency. The ideological basis of this outlook lay in human capital theory which achieved intellectual dominance in the 1960s in both Britain and America. It was, in fact, Theodore W. Schultz's Presidential Address to the American Economic Association in 1960 on the theme 'Investment in Human Capital' that was to have such a profound influence on a whole generation of sociologists and economists. Schultz's message was simple and straightforward: the process of acquiring skills and knowledge through education was to be viewed not as a form of consumption, but rather as a productive investment. 'By investing in themselves, people can enlarge the range of choice available to them. It is the one way free men can enhance their welfare' (Schultz, 1961, p.2). As Schultz went on to make clear, investment in human capital not only increases individual productivity, but, in so doing, also lays the technical base of the type of labour force necessary for rapid economic growth. And this superficially attractive message secured keen converts across the whole political spectrum. As Karabel and Halsey have pointed out, it even made a direct appeal to pro-capitalist ideological sentiment through its insistence that:

> the worker is a *holder of capital* (as embodied in his skills and knowledge) and that he has the *capacity to invest* (in himself). Thus in a single bold conceptual stroke, the *wage-earner,* who holds no property and controls neither the process nor the product of his labour, is transformed into a *capitalist* . . . We cannot be surprised, then, that a doctrine reaffirming the American way of life and offering quantitative justification for vast public expenditure on education should receive generous sponsorship in the United States (Karabel and Halsey, 1977, p.13).

In Britain between 1964 and 1970 variations of the theory possessed obvious attractions for a Labour Government committed more to piecemeal reform than to radical change. The twin watchwords were social equality and economic progress, though neither concept was ever defined too closely. As Hunter has observed:

> in a period of growing GNP, it was possible to support the two potentially opposing objectives; that secondary schooling should work towards creating greater social justice and equality within society *and* be an investment in creating a more efficient workforce (Hunter, 1984, p.274).

The same point was made by Wilby in a perceptive and illuminating article in the *New Statesman* in September 1977:

> It is frequently suggested that designing education for equality and designing
> education for national wealth are somehow opposed, that once we have called
> off our romance with the former, we can get on unsentimentally with the latter.
> On the contrary, the belief that education would prime economic growth was an
> essential element in the liberal faith that more education would mean more equality.
> The two ideas were really one idea (Wilby, 1977, p.358).

At the same time, in Wilby's view, educational reform in the 1960s was seen
as a means of ameliorating the more brutal inequalities in society, or at least
producing a greater degree of social harmony, without in any way disturbing
the basic class structure of the capitalist system:

> Educational equality was an attempt to achieve social change by proxy. More and
> better education was more politically palatable and less socially disruptive than
> direct measures of tackling inequality. So was economic growth. Even the most
> complacently privileged could hardly object to children attending better schools
> and to the nation producing more wealth. Equality of educational opportunity
> had an altogether more agreeable ring to it than any other form of equality, such
> as equality of income or equality of property. With its overtones of self-
> improvement, it could even appeal to the more conservative elements in society.
> Its beauty was that, while many must gain, it did not imply that any must lose.
> Ugly words such as redistribution and expropriation did not apply to education
> — or nobody thought they applied. Education was a cornucopia, so prolific of
> good things that nobody would need any longer to ask awkward questions about
> who got what (ibid.).

It can be argued, then, that the comprehensive reform in this country was,
in part at least, a response to profound conservative instincts. And this may
help to explain why in many areas it was not accompanied by radical changes
in curriculum content and pedagogy. The movement which gathered
momentum after the promulgation of Circular 10/65 in 1965 — based on
the pioneering work of certain 'progressive' local authorities in the 1950s
and supported by a modest crop of middle-class pressure groups — attracted
converts with a wide variety of aims and aspirations. This was always a source
both of strength and of weakness: ensuring strong local support for a vast
number of first-class genuine comprehensive schools but, at the same time,
preventing the comprehensive movement as a whole from establishing its
own clearly-defined criteria of success. It is certainly clear, as Simon has
argued, that the transition to comprehensive education was seen to be
'necessary', in some senses at least, 'for the maintenance and smooth

functioning of the existing social order' (Simon, 1978, p.30). It was widely believed, particularly among reformist elements in the Labour Party, that the new system would *both* reduce the wastage of the human abilities so urgently required as a result of technological change and economic advance *and* ensure an amelioration of social class differences through the pupils' experience of 'social mixing' in a common environment. Yet there were many, including, of course, Simon himself, who demanded the transition from a quite different and far more positive standpoint: namely a belief in the educability of *all* children and in the futility of forcing them into outworn categories.

Few argued for the comprehensive reform along lines that were specifically related to curriculum change. In the new schools which developed in the 1960s, with a few notable exceptions, the expectations of parents, the demands of the examination system and the competition from neighbouring grammar schools tended to reinforce an emphasis on the acquisition of cognitive-intellectual skills. Influential members of the Labour Party had, after all, promoted comprehensive schools as ensuring a 'grammar-school education for all'. And there was a very real sense in which, to begin with at least, many comprehensive schools *did* become the new grammar schools in that they allowed themselves to be dominated by the grammar-school curriculum. In the words of Elliott: 'through the growth of comprehensive reorganization and people's attempts to legitimate it in terms of a grammar-school education for all, secondary education in Britain became "grammarized"' (Elliott, 1983, p.119).

As late as 1979, a survey of secondary education by Her Majesty's Inspectors of Schools showed that the examinable academic subjects still occupied the heart of the comprehensive school curriculum to the detriment of both able and less-able pupils:

It was evident that in some schools pupils were being entered for examinations inappropriate to their particular abilities and some embarked on examination courses who would have been better suited by non-examination courses. Elsewhere, the range of programmes offered to some groups of pupils, usually the more able, was narrowed: these pupils were thought to have no time to spare for creative and aesthetic subjects and non-examination courses. Careers education, health education and religious eduction also tended to be excluded. The work attempted in the classroom was often constrained by exclusive emphasis placed on the examination syllabus, on the topics thought to be favoured by the examiners and on the acquisition of examination techniques. In almost all the schools no time was made available in the fourth and fifth years for reflective work such as might be fostered by independent but carefully guided private study periods and the development of study skills which the pupils might need later in school, or for future education or employment. The pupils may be put at a disadvantage by this narrowing of their curricula and modes of work and the ensuing effects on the range of skills, values and attitudes which they have acquired. Certainly, some pupils responded by showing little interest in anything which was not seen to be related to their examination work. Other pupils, for example those leaving at Easter in the fifth year or not intended to take examination courses, may also be at a disadvantage in schools where the examination objective has such primacy (DES, 1979, p.217).

By the time this survey was published, the education system in this country was experiencing a profound lack of direction. The period of the 1970s saw the demise of the old confident liberal dogmas. Expansion and optimism had given way to contraction and doubt.

The policy-makers of the 1960s had seen a direct and indisputable correlation between educational reform and economic prosperity: a skilled and educated workforce would facilitate economic growth which would, in turn, constitute a firm basis for continuing educational expansion. But by the mid 1970s, the post-war consensus was breaking down on a number of fronts. As Tony Benn has observed:

> The post-war consensus, built upon full employment and the welfare state, has failed to command the support of people because they have seen first that it did not contain within it any element whatsoever of transformation, and, secondly, that even by its own criteria it failed. That policy could not bring about growth, it could not extend freedom, it could not even maintain let alone develop welfare and it could not sustain full employment (Benn, 1980, p.6).

As far as the economy was concerned, both in Britain and throughout the Western world, the crucial years were 1973-5. The major world recession that erupted in 1974-5 marked the decisive end of what Gamble has described as 'the longest and most rapid period of continuous expansion world capitalism has ever enjoyed' (Gamble, 1985, p.6). The period 1971-3 had seen a sharp boom in each of the major advanced capitalist countries and a generally rising rate of inflation. Some downturn, it could be argued, was likely to occur in 1974 or 1975 simply as part of the usual rhythm of the business cycle. However, in the event, the generality and depth of the recession was unprecedented in the post-war period and can now be seen as marking the end of the long expansionary phase of post-war accumulation (Currie, 1983, p.89). While it would, of course, be wrong to see the recession as having a single cause, its onset was clearly marked by a very big rise in the price of oil in 1973. And the economic difficulties of Western societies in the years that followed served to challenge the liberal and expansionist beliefs of the 1960s. As Bernbaum has pointed out (Bernbaum, 1979, p.12): 'if economies are no longer characterized by high rates of growth, then the assumptions that growth is closely related to the benefits obtained through large-scale educational enterprises are more readily challenged'. At the same time, a declining birth-rate in Britain and elsewhere has made the educational budget a relatively easy target in the drive to reduce the expenditure of local and national governments.

It can be argued (see, for example, Ramsay and Dorril, 1986) that there were two major complementary trends influencing political developments in Britain in the 1970s, or, to be more precise, between 1973 and 1979. On the one hand, right-wing elements within the Conservative Party and groups beyond it were working to destroy first Edward Heath, then the Labour Governments of Harold Wilson and James Callaghan, in order to prepare the way for the arrival of a right-wing Thatcher Government. At the same time, the leadership of the Labour Party was steadily losing its nerve and seeking to stem the tide of Conservative advance by the adoption of right-wing rhetoric and policies.

According to this analysis, James Callaghan's Ruskin College Speech of October 1976, with its concern for standards and a better understanding between schools and industry, can be seen as a thinly-disguised attempt to wrest the populist mantle from the Conservatives and pander to perceived public disquiet at the alleged prevalence of soft-centred progressivism. And the subsequent Green Paper, published in July 1977, made it clear that in launching the Great Debate, the Government had been well aware of the media campaign against the state education system:

> The speech was made against a background of strongly critical comment in the press and elsewhere on education and educational standards. Children's standards of performance in their school work were said to have declined. The curriculum, it was argued, paid too little attention to the basic skills of reading, writing and arithmetic, and was overloaded with fringe subjects. Teachers lacked adequate professional skills, and did not know how to discipline children or to instil in them concern for hard work or good manners. Underlying all this was the feeling that the educational system was out of touch with the fundamental need for Britain to survive economically in a highly competitive world through the efficiency of its industry and commerce (DES, 1977a, p.2).

At the same time, as Callaghan has revealed in his recent book of memoirs, *Time and Chance,* he had good reasons for wanting to stress his and Labour's commitment to social issues at a time when the centre of the stage was commandeered by economic disasters and the demise of the Government was being forecast with frightening regularity (Callaghan, 1987, pp.397-8, 408-12).

By highlighting 1976 as something of a turning-point in education, one avoids the common mistake of seeing Thatcherism as a major break in social policy. In education, as in so many other aspects of social and economic policy, Thatcherism (the basic ideology of the Conservative Governments in power since 1979) can be viewed as a logical extension of the policies pursued by the Callaghan administration (Gamble, 1985, p.193). The ten years that have elapsed since the Ruskin College Speech and the so-called Great Debate have been notable for a number of trends and developments which give the period a peculiar unity and can be collected together under *four* main headings: differentiation; vocationalization; centralization; and privatization.

Differentiation

As Secretary of State for Education from 1976-9, Shirley Williams believed firmly in the principle of parental choice. She argued that within the state system, there should be a variety of provision with no concession to the concept of 'neighbourhood' or 'community' schools. In a pamphlet published in 1977, her Conservative opposite number, Norman St. John-Stevas, praised her for her sensible, non-doctrinaire approach to education:

> There are signs that in some respects the political parties are moving closer together on educational matters. I welcome the conversion of Mr Callaghan and Mrs Williams to much of what the Conservative Party has been saying on standards and parental rights and influence. That is all to the good. Mrs Williams, if a free agent, would clearly return to an older Labour tradition which lays stress, not on impossible equalities, but on high standards, academic excellence, and the importance of providing a ladder of opportunity for the bright child from a disadvantaged home (St. John-Stevas, 1977 p.9).

Seven years later, in 1984, Sir Keith Joseph (Education Secretary from 1981 to 1986) had to acknowledge the failure of attempts to reintroduce selection in Solihull and elsewhere. Questioned by Brian Walden on ITV's *Weekend World* programme, he stressed the need for different educational routes *within* the comprehensive school. 'If it be so, as it is, that selection *between* schools is largely out', he said, apparently conceding defeat on this issue, 'then I emphasize that there *must* be differentiation *within* schools' (reported in *The Times Educational Supplement,* 17 February 1984).

In fact, of course, even at the time of this revealing *Weekend World* interview, there was still a considerable degree of differentiation *between* schools. Even in Solihull itself, the comprehensive system was based on clearly-defined catchment areas which served to ensure that local or 'community' schools meant schools serving a relatively homogeneous social class intake. As Walford and Jones have pointed out in a recent article (1986, p.251), children from the affluent middle-class areas in the south of the borough were well catered for, attending prestigious schools well supported by active parent-teacher associations. There was certainly no social mixing with the Birmingham overspill children living in the north of the borough. And in a BBC TV *Panorama* programme, 'Schools: selling the children short', shown in March 1986, Margaret Jay pointed to the three-tier structure of secondary schools that had developed in many areas: a top tier consisting of well-endowed, well resourced private schools, a middle tier embracing comprehensive schools with prosperous middle-class catchment areas and parents able to find money for expensive books and equipment, and a bottom tier where school buildings were crumbling and books were scarce.

In the last five years, the TVEI (Technical and Vocational Education Initiative), funded from outside education by the Manpower Services Commission, and the DES-funded LAPP (Lower Attaining Pupils Programme) for the so-called 'bottom 40 per cent' can be seen as further attempts to introduce differentiation into the system (Chitty, 1986; Hutchinson, 1986; Weston, 1986). And the new GCSE is not proving to be the common examination so many educationalists and teachers have campaigned for since 1966. What we are getting is not a single examination but a system of examinations (with the GCE boards responsible for the higher grades and the old CSE boards for the lower grades) with differentiated examination papers and/or questions in many, if not most, subjects. As Gipps has observed in a recent Bedford Way Paper:

> Differentiation means that the system will still be divisive: that there will be separate routes to the examination; that some candidates will not be eligible for higher grades (if they take the less difficult route); that teachers will still have to decide which students are suited for which route/course/range of grades; that in some cases these decisions will still have to be made as early as fourteen (Gipps, 1986, p.15).

It is also worth noting that the concept of differentiated papers first appeared as DES policy in a Government White Paper in 1978, during Shirley Williams's period as Education Secretary, where one of the recommendations was 'to ensure that alternative papers are used wherever this is necessary to maintain standards' (DES, 1978, p.11).

The concept of a unified or common curriculum for those aged eleven to sixteen, as outlined, for example, in *Curriculum 11-16* (1977) and *A View of the Curriculum* (1980), both incorporating the thoughts of Her Majesty's Inspectorate, seems now to have been quietly dropped. It became fashionable in the early years of this decade to talk in terms of a natural break at fourteen and of new approaches to the curriculum for the fourteen-to-eighteen or fourteen-to-sixteen age range. In 1983, the Youth Education Service produced *Implementing the 14-18 Curriculum: new approaches* by Brockington, White and Pring. And this was followed by an updated, revised and expanded edition, *The 14-18 Curriculum: integrating CPVE, YTS, TVEI?*, which was published in January 1985. In February 1986, the Standing Conference of Regional Examination Boards (which was disbanded in October 1986) produced *An Alternative Approach to the Curriculum 14-16*. And the Further Education Unit (FEU) has made its own contribution to the debate by producing *Supporting Vocational Change*, a revised and updated version of both *A Basis for Choice*, first published in June 1979, and *Vocational Preparation* published in 1981. In this revised document, published in 1987, vocational preparation is defined as 'the supportive process of education/training, relevant to the aspirations and potential of individuals, necessary to accompany vocational and/or occupational change' and it is suggested as an entitlement for all people aged over fourteen (FEU, 1987). Then again, the Inner London Education Authority's Hargreaves Report on *Improving Secondary Schools*, published in March 1984, the Oxford Certificate of Educational Achievement (OCEA) and the Manchester Assessment Project (MAP) can all be seen as part of an attempt to redefine and reform educational pedagogy and process for the fourteen-to-eighteen age range. And of crucial significance here is the work being done on the advantages and disadvantages of a modular approach to the curriculum and timetable for fourth-, fifth- and sixth- year pupils (see, for example, York, 1986; Watkins, 1987).

There is clearly much of value being proposed in what Ranson, Taylor and Brighouse (1986, pp.1-10) call 'the new education'. It rejects selection either of students or of curriculum content while, at the same time, seeking to design learning experiences which meet the needs of each young person or adult.

The new education argues that traditional schooling has been straight-jacketed by an unduly limited conception of academic achievement. Passing exams may not adequately test cognitive skills, let alone assess other aspects of personal development. By celebrating practical, creative and social skills, the new pedagogy seeks to acknowledge and to reinforce the diversity of human capacity. There is an important attempt here to redefine what counts as achievement . . . The new education pursues a policy of whole curriculum planning for whole people and seeks to weaken the boundaries between areas of experience so as to integrate the curriculum (ibid., p.3).

But this is not the whole story; for alongside these interesting developments have come attempts to make differentiation a marked feature of the provision for the fourteen-to-eighteen clientele.

The White Paper, *Better Schools,* published in March 1985, acknowledged that the new GCSE, with its first candidates in 1988, would be only one of a number of examinations competing for the custom of aspiring sixteen-year-olds:

> Some schools prepare pupils for pre-vocational examinations other than O level and CSE (e.g. those of the City and Guilds of London Institute, the Royal Society of Arts, and the Business and Technician Education Council) during the years of compulsory schooling. Such courses will continue to be available to complement GCSE examinations as well, in the service of a curriculum which is broad, balanced, relevant, and differentiated in accordance with pupil's abilities (DES, 1985, p.32).

The White Paper went on to announce the setting up of a working party 'to draft national criteria for pre-vocational and vocationally oriented examination courses taken by pupils of statutory school age'. The working party would also be asked to consider progression from such courses to post-sixteen courses leading to vocational qualifications. It spent a year on its tasks and produced its report, the Johnson Report, in June 1986, but its terms of reference were severely criticized by the FEU which argued that the Report's preoccupation with single-subject courses had led to an emphasis on the examinable parts of the curriculum, to the neglect of other crucial aspects (reported in *The Times Educational Supplement,* 12 December 1986).

At the same time, the Joint Board for Pre-Vocational Education, set up in May 1983 to administer the new Certificate of Pre-Vocational Education (CPVE), was preparing its own plans for the fourteen-to-eighteen age range. A press release was issued in January 1984 to announce that:

> BTEC (the Business and Technician Education Council) and CGLI (City and Guilds of London Institute) see their decision to adopt a joint approach to pre-

vocational education as a major contribution to helping schools ànd colleges provide young people with a more effective transition from school to work. The two bodies want to create a new curriculum pathway for that majority of those between the ages of fourteen and eighteen for whom the traditional academic curriculum is unsuitable.

This was followed by a further statement in September 1985 announcing that:

> the Councils of BTEC and City and Guilds have agreed jointly to develop and operate a new pre-vocational provision for students aged fourteen to sixteen which will offer a national alternative to traditional subject-based school courses.

And these have resulted in the publication in May 1986 of *The Framework Description of BTEC-City and Guilds Pre-Vocational Programmes for Pupils Aged 14-16* incorporating the different existing programmes, City and Guilds 365 and Foundation Courses and BTEC Preparatory Programmes, into one common framework.

If present trends continue, there seems little cause for optimism that the term 'comprehensive education' will actually come to mean anything beyond the age of fourteen. While bodies such as the Joint Board are allowed to peddle their wares alongside GCSE, the concept of differentiation assumes a new and permanent significance. At the same time, the increased prevalence of pre-vocational courses for the fourteen-to sixteen age range will clearly have severe implications for the future development of the CPVE. A pre-vocational curriculum for large numbers of students *before* the age of sixteen obviously means less need for the CPVE at sixteen-plus. And it will also produce increased repetition of learning for particular groups of under-achieving students and their enforced marginalization as they proceed through the system.

Not that the age of fourteen is necessarily thought to be early enough for the process of differentiation to begin in schools. Education Secretary Kenneth Baker and Employment Secretary Lord Young were quoted in June 1986 as agreeing that 'greater emphasis must be placed in schools on vocational training from the age of eleven — at least for less bright pupils — to give them a better chance of finding work'. This would mean, they argued, that 'academic school work would be afforded a lower priority for the less bright and that more "training for work" classes would be encouraged' (Cochrane, 1986). And in his *Weekend World* television interview at the beginning of December 1986, the Education Secretary argued that education for 'the bottom 40 per cent' should be more vocational from the age of eleven or twelve. Which brings us on to the second theme of the last ten years.

Vocationalization

In his Ruskin College Speech, James Callaghan argued that schools were failing, in that youngsters were not being trained in the skills necessary to find employment in industry and commerce:

> I am concerned on my journeys to find complaints from industry that new recruits from the schools sometimes do not have the basic tools to do the job that is required . . . The goals of our education, from nursery school through to adult education, are clear enough. They are to equip children to the best of their ability for a lively, constructive place in society and also to fit them to do a job of work. Not one or the other; but both . . . There is no virtue in producing socially well-adjusted members of society who are unemployed because they do not have the skills (reprinted in *Education*, 22 October 1976, pp.332-3).

Here we have a classic statement of the 'skills-deficit model' of unemployment which argues that one of the key factors in the rise of unemployment is the shortage of relevant skills. Schools and teachers can then be blamed for failing to teach those skills (whatever they may be) which would make their students more employable.

The same emphasis on the reluctance of schools to train pupils to meet the needs of wealth-producing industry is evident in the subsequent Green Paper published in July 1977. Here reference is made to the criticisms voiced at the regional conferences which followed the Ruskin Speech:

> It was said that the school system is geared to promote the importance of academic learning and careers with the result that pupils, especially the more able, are prejudiced against work in productive industry and trade; that teachers lack experience, knowledge and understanding of trade and industry; that curricula are not related to the realities of most pupils' work after leaving school; and that pupils leave school with little or no understanding of the workings, or importance, of the wealth-producing sector of our economy (DES, 1977a, p.34).

The Department of Employment White Paper, *A New Training Initiative: a programme for action,* published in December 1981, reaffirmed, without reservation, a strictly utilitarian view of education and training:

> To get a better trained and more flexible workforce, we need to start with better preparation for working life in schools and better opportunities for continuing education and personal development in the early years at work . . . The last two years of compulsory education are particularly important in forming an approach to the world of work. Every pupil needs to be helped to reach his or her full potential, not only for personal development but to prepare for the whole range

of demands which employment will make. The Government is seeking to ensure that the school curriculum develops the personal skills and qualities as well as the knowledge needed for working life, and that links between schools and employers help pupils and teachers to gain a closer understanding of the industrial, commercial and economic base of our society (D of E, 1982, p.5).

This was, of course one of the key documents leading to the launching of the Youth Training Scheme (YTS) in September 1983.

The Technical and Vocational Education Initiative (TVEI), launched by Margaret Thatcher in a Commons written statement in November 1982, was designed, in the words of the accompanying Department of Employment press release, 'to stimulate technical and vocational education for fourteen-to-eighteen year olds as part of a drive to improve our performance in the development of new skills and technology'. It was also seen as a follow-up to the 1981 White Paper in acknowledging 'the importance of the last two years of compulsory education and the need for more vocationally-orientated courses for those continuing full-time education past sixteen' (D of E, 1981, p.1). In a letter to all LEA Directors of Education in England and Wales in January 1983, David (now Lord) Young, the then Chairman of the Manpower Services Commission, stated that the primary objective of the TVEI was 'to widen and enrich the curriculum in a way that will help young people to prepare for the world of work' (Young, 1983, p.2).

The philosophy of the DES and MSC for the large majority of youngsters of secondary school age and beyond is often described both as 'the new vocationalism' and as 'narrow vocationalism' (see, for examples, Bates et al., 1984); but, as Green has argued (1986, p.102), neither term is really adequate since the policy is neither 'vocationalist' nor 'narrow' in a traditional training sense:

> Vocational education has normally meant preparation for a particular job and its connotations of 'calling' are clearly tied up with a Protestant work ethic and the middle-class preoccupation with choosing a career. Youth training schemes, however, are explicitly concerned with training for work in general and not preparation for a particular job, and there is precious little real choice for most young people involved. Furthermore one of the defining characteristics of youth training is that it does involve broad-based skills training and specifically eschews skill specialization. Although it may be 'narrow' in other, and especially, educational senses, the use of the term would be confusing in the training context.

Green's comments are equally applicable to the thinking behind the courses currently being advocated for the fourteen-to-sixteen age range, and particularly for those who are not thought capable of a range of GCSE passes. What matters now is the cultivation of adaptability and the willingness of young people to accept the fact that many working lives are likely to consist of a succession of unskilled jobs. Parry Rogers, Chairman of the Institute of Directors and newly-appointed Chairman of B/TEC, has recently urged teachers that 'all young people should be prepared for a working life in which they will change skills and occupations several times' (Rogers, 1987, p.18). And the DES document *Better Schools,* published in 1985, lays enormous stress on the need for a work-force which is versatile, adaptable, highly motivated and productive:

> It is vital that schools should always remember that preparation for working life is one of their principal functions. The economic stresses of our time and the pressures of international competition make it more necessary than ever before that Britain's work-force should possess the skills and attitudes, and display the understanding, the enterprise and adaptability that the pervasive impact of technological advance will increasingly demand (DES, 1985, p.15).

It is hard to avoid the conclusion that, despite the fine phrases, we are witnessing the conversion of education into a servicing-process for a free enterprise economy.

Centralization and privatization
Once again, analysis must begin with Callaghan's Ruskin College Speech of October 1976. The Prime Minister was anxious to repudiate the suggestion that education policy in general and curriculum policy in particular could be said to be the exclusive concern of any one group:

> If everything is reduced to such phrases as: 'educational freedom versus State control', we shall get nowhere . . . Parents, teachers, learned and professional bodies, representatives of higher education and both sides of industry, together with the Government, all have an important part to play in formulating and expressing the purpose of education and the standards that we need.

As a *Times* leader writer pointed out (27 June 1977), this speech gave the DES the initiative to develop a policy of change from the centre.

The Prime Minister's sentiments were echoed by his Secretary of State, Shirley Williams, in a speech at Rockingham College of Further Education a few days after the Ruskin address:

> Among the splendours of the English system are its flexibility, its imagination,

and the freedom of the teacher in the classroom. No one wishes to jeopardize that. But the curriculum is a matter in which many people have a stake: parents, teachers, employers, trade unions, Parliament, and of course, the Government itself. We have, through discussion and debate, to produce the most satisfactory curricula we can (quoted in NUT, 1977, p.4).

Between 1976 and 1981, a stream of documents on the curriculum flowed from the DES, those emanating from HMI advocating an 'areas of experience' approach and those representing the bureaucratic viewpoint arguing for a compulsory 'core' consisting of a limited range of subjects. Then, suddenly, the DES bureaucrats seemed to tire of the politics of persuasion. It has been argued (Nuttall, 1984; Maw, 1985; Chitty, 1986) that, having failed in their attempts to determine what was taught in schools through documents like *A Framework for the School Curriculum* (1980) and *The School Curriculum* (1981), they simply decided to try to achieve their aims by other means, notably the instigation of examination reforms. It is, of course, significant that the new CPVE and the proposed A levels emanate from the DES, and criteria for the new GCSE are vetted there. This argument has certainly been supported by Sir James Hamilton who was Permanent Secretary at the DES from 1976 to 1983. Looking back over those years, he argued at a conference organized by the Association for Science Education that the Government had generally shown too much 'delicacy' about making its presence felt in the classroom:

I believe we erred on the side of safety. I believe that we could, with benefit, have produced a more pungent, a more purposive analysis . . . There is an argument for the DES acting more directly in certain limited areas of the curriculum . . . . The present exercise of reforming examinations at sixteen-plus should be seen as part of this process of establishing greater central control (reported in *The Times Educational Supplement*, 1 July 1983).

Other examples of the centralizing process would include: the abolition of the Schools Council in January 1984 (see Plaskow, 1985); the control of teacher education through the introduction of the Council for the Accreditation of Teacher Education; the control of in-service training for teachers by means of a specific grant, as outlined in *Better Schools* (1985, p.54); and the introduction of education support grants under the terms of the 1984 Education Act and as part of the shift towards categorical funding. Most important of all is the recent announcement by Kenneth Baker (7 April 1987) of plans for the introduction of a national core curriculum setting uniform standards in schools (Lawton, 1987; Lawton and Chitty, 1987).

Paradoxically, plans to bring about greater central control of education appear to be moving ahead alongside plans to privatize the service. Here at last are signs of a real break with past traditions. When Kenneth Baker replaced Sir Keith Joseph in May 1986 and dispensed with the services of Stuart Sexton — Sir Keith's special adviser and the high priest of education vouchers and free-market conomics — it was confidently expected that the moderates and bureaucrats would consolidate their control of the DES. But this has not proved to be the case. If one sees the central authority as a 'tension system', not as a consensus (Lawton, 1984; 1986), it could be argued that Baker has become the willing puppet of that right-wing group both inside and outside the DES which would dearly love to see large areas of the state system dismantled. If, for example, the new City Technology Colleges are to be regarded as 'prototypes' for the entire secondary system — independent of LEA control and able to recruit as many pupils as they can — they might well be a first step on the road to the surrender of education to crude market forces (Chitty, 1987).

All this might appear to paint a very depressing and negative picture of the current educational scene. It remains, of course, to be seen, as the country embarks on its third period of Conservative rule under Margaret Thatcher, which of the two views within what has become mainstream Conservative philosophy and within the DES itself will prevail: the bureaucratic view seeking to establish central control of the system or the view of the so-called New Right anxious to see the ownership of schools transferred from local authorities to individual trusts. It has been argued (Wilby, 1987) that even Sir Keith Joseph came to accept that a 'market' in compulsory education was a logical impossibility. How ironic, then, that the idea should be revived in a new form under his 'moderate' successor. A likely outcome will be a mixed system; and Baker has himself said that he would welcome this. In a recent discussion with Stuart Maclure (Maclure, 1987), he argued for a system where the new City Technology Colleges would act as a sort of 'halfway house' between state schools and the independent sector: 'I would like to see many more halfway houses, a greater choice, a greater variety'.

Somehow teachers have got to find a way of working *within* the new system with all its in-built tensions and harmful contradictions. In the final chapter of this Paper — and drawing upon the observations of other contributors — I shall seek to show that, despite the ideological standpoint of those initiating change, real advance can still be made *within* the structures being erected by the New Right.

References

Bates, I. et al. (1984), *Schooling for the Dole? The new vocationalism.* London: Macmilliam.

Benn, T. (1980), Interview with Eric Hobsbawm, *Marxism Today,* October.

Bernbaum, G. (1979), Editorial Introduction to: Bernbaum (ed.), *Schooling in Decline.* London: Macmillan, pp.1-16.

Brockington, D., White, R. and Pring, R. (1983), *Implementing the 14-18 Curriculum: New Approaches,* The Youth Education Service, Bristol Social Education Project, Schools Council Publications.

_____ (1985), *The 14-18 Curriculum: Integrating CPVE, YTS, TVEI?* The Youth Education Service.

Callaghan, J. (1987), *Time and Chance,* London: Collins.

Chitty, C. (1986), 'TVEI: The MSC's Trojan Horse', in C. Benn and J. Fairley, (eds.), *Challenging the MSC: on jobs, education and training.* London: Pluto Press, pp.76-98.

_____ (1987), 'City Technology Colleges: the commodification of education', *Forum,* Vol. 29, No. 3, Summer, pp.66-69.

Cochrane, A. (1986), 'Wet-dry axis on education', *Sunday Telegraph,* 15 June.

Currie D. (1983), 'World capitalism in recession', in S. Hall and M. Jacques (eds.), *The Politics of Thatcherism.* London: Lawrence and Wishart, pp. 79-105.

DES (1977a), *Education in Schools: a consultative document* (Green Paper), London: HMSO, Cmnd. 6869.

_____ (1977b), *Curriculum 11-16* (HMI Red Book One), London: HMSO.

_____ (1978), *Secondary School Examinations: a single system at 16-plus* (White Paper), London: HMSO, Cmnd. 7368

_____ (1979,) *Aspects of Secondary Education in England: A Survey by HM Inspectors of Schools,* London: HMSO.

_____ (1980a), *A Framework for the School Curriculum,* London: HMSO.

_____ (1980b), *A View of the Curriculum*, HMI Series 'Matters for Discussion' No. 11, London: HMSO.

_____ (1981) *The School Curriculum*, London: HMSO.

_____ (1985) *Better Schools*, London: HMSO, Cmnd. 9469.

DofE (1981), *A New Training Initiative: A Programme for Action*, London: HMSO, Cmnd. 8455.

_____ (1982), Press Notice: 'New technical education initiative', 12 November.

Elliott, J. (1983), 'A curriculum for the study of human affairs: the contribution of Lawrence Stenhouse', *Journal of Curriculum Studies*, Vol. 15, No. 2, pp.105-23.

FEU (1979; second edition, 1982), *A Basis for Choice*, London: DES.

_____ (1981), *Vocational Preparation*, London: DES.

_____ (1987), *Supporting Vocational Change*, London: DES.

Gamble, A. (1981, 1985), *Britain in Decline: Economic Policy, Political Strategy and the British State*, London: Macmillan.

Gipps, C. (1986), 'GCSE: some background', in C. Gipps (ed.) *The GCSE: An Uncommon Examination*, Bedford Way Paper 29, University of London Institute of Education.

Green, A. (1986), 'The MSC and the three-tier structure of further education', in C. Benn and J. Fairley (eds.), *Challenging the MSC: on jobs, education and training*, London: Pluto Press, pp.99-122.

Gregory, J. (1987), 'Comprehensive comrades', *The Times Educational Supplement*, 6 February.

Hunter, C. (1984), 'The political devaluation of comprehensives: what of the future?', in S. Ball (ed.), *Comprehensive Schooling: a reader*. Lewes: Falmer Press, pp.273-292.

Hutchinson, B. (1986), 'The public image of a DES Lower Attaining Pupils' Programme initiative in a local education authority', *Cambridge Journal of Education*, Vol. 16, No. 2, Summer, pp.100-116.

ILEA (1984), *Improving Secondary Schools: Report of the Committee on the Curriculum and Organization of Secondary Schools* (The Hargreaves Report), London: ILEA, March.

Joint Unit for 14-16 Pre-Vocational Education (1986), *BTEC — City and Guilds Pre-Vocational Programmes for Pupils Aged 14-16: the Framework Description*, May.

Karabel, J. and Halsey, A. H. (1977), 'Educational research: a review and an Interpretation', in Karabel and Halsey (eds.) *Power and Ideology in Education.* New York: Oxford University Press, pp.1-85.

Lawton, D. (1984), *The Tightening Grip: Growth of Central Control of the School Curriculum*, Bedford Way Paper 21, University of London Institute of Education.

————— (1986), 'The Department of Education and Science: policy-making at the centre', in A. Hartnett and M. Naish (eds.), *Education and Society Today*, Lewes: Falmer Press, pp.19-36.

————— (1987), 'Cutting the curriculum cloth', *The Times Educational Supplement*, 1 May.

Lawton, D. and Chitty, C. (1987), 'Towards a national curriculum' *Forum*, Vol. 30, No. 1 Autumn.

Maclure, S. (1987), 'Leading from the centre', *The Times Educational Supplement*, 3 April.

Maw, J. (1985), 'Curriculum control and cultural norms: change and conflict in a British context', *The New Era*, Vol. 66, No. 4, pp.95-8.

NUT (National Union of Teachers) (1977), *Education: The Great Debate.*

Nuttall, D. (1984), 'Doomsday or a new dawn? The prospects for a common system of examining at 16-plus', in P. Broadfoot (ed.), *Selection, Certification and Control: social issues in educational assessment*, Lewes: Falmer Press, pp.163-77.

Plaskow, M. (1985), *Life and Death of the Schools Council*, Lewes: Falmer Press.

Ramsay, R. and Dorril, S. (1986), 'Wilson, MI5 and the rise of Thatcher: covert operations in British politics, 1974-78', *The Lobster* No. 11, April.

Ranson, S., Taylor, B. and Brighouse, T. (1986), 'A Janus-headed revolution in education and training', in Ranson, Taylor and Brighouse (eds.), *The Revolution in Education and Training*. Harlow: Longman, pp.1-10.

Reynolds, D., Sullivan, M. and Murgatroyd, S. (1987), *The Comprehensive Experiment: a comparison of the selective and non-selective system of school organization:* Lewes: Falmer Press.

Rogers, P. (1987), 'Vocational education: first define the task', *Manpower Policy and Practice,* Vol. 2, No. 3, Spring, pp.17-18.

St. John-Stevas, N. (1977), *Better Schools For All: a Conservative approach to the problems of the comprehensive school,* London: Conservative Political Centre.

Schultz, T. (1961), 'Investment in human capital' *American Economic Review* 51, March, pp.1-17.

Simon, B. (1978), 'Problems in contemporary educational theory: a Marxist approach', *Journal of Philosophy of Education,* Vol. 12, pp.29-39.

Social Trends 16 (1986), London: HMSO.

Standing Conference of Regional Examinations Boards (1986), *An Alternative Approach to the Curriculum 14-16: Report to the Steering Committee, February.*

Walford, G. and Jones, S. (1986), 'The Solihull adventure: an attempt to reintroduce selective schooling', *Journal of Education Policy,* Vol. 1, No. 3, July-September, pp.239-53.

Watkins, P. (1987), *Modular Approaches to the Secondary Curriculum,* Longman for the School Curriculum Development Committee.

Weston, P. (1986), 'If success had many faces: thinking about the Lower Attaining Pupils, Programme', *Forum,* Vol. 28, No. 3, Summer, pp.79-81.

Wilby, P. (1977), 'Education and equality', *New Statesman,* 16 September, pp.358-61.

———— (1987), 'Close-up: Kenneth Baker', *Marxism Today,* April.

York, A. (1986), *The Management, Organizational and Curricular Implications of the Implementation of a Modular Approach to the Curriculum and Timetable of Years Four, Five and Six,* Haringey Occasional Papers in Education No. 1, London Borough of Haringey, May.

Young, D. (1983), Circular to Directors of Education on Technical and Vocational Education Initiative.. Sheffield: MSC, 28 January.

Vocationalizing Tendencies in Recent British Educational Policy: sources of exclusion or sources of empowerment?

Michael Young

The theme of 'vocationalization' is a very broad one, both conceptually and empirically. Resting as it does on the basic tenets of human capital theory and functionalist sociology, it raises issues fundamental to the relationship between education and society in Western capitalist countries. It has its origins in the developing crisis of the economic productivity of British industry, and is an attempt to locate both the cause and the solution to that crisis in the country's system of education and training. In highlighting what is taken to be a failure of the education system to meet 'industrial needs' and all but a small academic elite's perception of individual needs, it is able to claim a resonance with popular consciousness, and to prescribe remedies which might in other circumstances have been controversial, as the inevitable movement of progress.

The changes which I shall discuss in this chapter, *have manifested themselves in the last ten years in a number of ways; I shall outline what the most significant have been:

1. An increasingly directive role for central government in implementing educational policy. This is particularly striking in England and Wales, because of the tradition of *local* autonomy in which the curriculum of each individual school has been the responsibility of its board of governors and teaching staff within *local* government guidelines. In practice this has meant inertia and resistance to change rather than significant innovations by individual schools; they are far too embedded in a culture of deference to university-controlled examination boards for that. The shift towards central government funding of its own curricular priorities is nothing less than an attack on the whole traditional framework of institutions and assumptions of the English and Welsh education system.

2. We have seen a shift in the focus of educational debate, both public and professional, from the issues of quantity and distribution of opportunities

*An earlier version of this paper appeared in *Bilding und Erziehung*, 1987, 1.

that have dominated policy discussions since the 1944 Education Act. The questioning, which most commentators see as beginning with the Ruskin College Speech of Prime Minister Callaghan in 1976, of the benefits of educational expansion, has been followed by an emphasis on quality and standards of provision, together with doubts about the existing ways schools are made accountable to the community.

3. Successive government policy statements have shown increasing disenchantment with the academic curriculum of separate school 'subjects', as the basis for defining the organization and content of educational knowledge for all pupils.

Empirically the changes, summarized under the theme vocationalization, are apparent in every sector and in the provision for every age group, from the funding priorities for universities to the encouragement of an 'enterprise culture' in primary schools. This chapter makes no claims to a comprehensive coverage. It will concentrate on those policy changes which bear most directly on the age group 14-18. For reasons which illustrate the weakness of the theoretical framework of human capital theory and functionalist sociology, this age group has been the major focus of policy initiatives. Though widely accepted by policy makers and social scientists in the 1960s, such theories could not have predicted the economic recession of the early 1970s nor the dramatic rise in unemployment that was its most serious consequence. The virtual disappearance of apprenticeship and the youth labour market has dominated educational policy initiatives and taken the major part of new funding, as *ad hoc* schemes for a youth opportunities programme have grown into the two-year national Youth Training Scheme. This focus of policy on providing alternatives to youth unemployment has highlighted a distinct feature of the UK system — the large number of pupils who, until the establishment of YTS, left school at sixteen (either for a job or unemployment) and never had any further experience of school (or college or formal training).

In the rest of this chapter, following a very brief sketch of the historical context of UK policy, I shall first describe the major changes as they affect the 14-18 age group. Secondly, I shall review a number of recent critical studies which have examined the consequences of these changes. Finally, I shall examine what I take to be certain contradictions in the process of vocationalization and its conceptualization as it is becoming manifest in the UK context, and suggest some possibilities for the establishment of a truly comprehensive tertiary system of post-16 education.

The context

The depth of the economic recession in Britain, which resulted largely from the rise in oil prices in the early 1970s has to be understood in terms of the peculiarities of the process of British industrialization. Far more than other countries, it depended on the fruits of imperialism: access to cheap raw materials (and in some cases, cheap labour) from the colonies. The industries of early industrialization (steel, coal, engineering and textiles) grew without any systematic investment in education and training, and in parallel with a highly elitist culture and university education geared to colonial administration and the home Civil Service rather than industrial production or technological innovation. The legacy of this period was commented on many times before the recent recession; however it is only since the mid-1970s, that the English academic tradition has been highlighted as itself responsible for the country's industrial decline. Policies for vocationalizing the curriculum are, then, in part, an attempt to counter a narrowly academic tradition which has been the model for this country's comprehensive secondary schools.

Attempts to relate education to industry need to be understood in relation to the form and persistence of wider social inequalities. Historically, vocational links between education and work have been close and specific only in relation to apprenticeships for a limited number of 'skilled' trades. Many sectors such as the hotel and retail trades have had no such connections. For the bulk of working-class occupations (often, in fact, requiring considerable skills and knowledge) no specific training has been seen as necessary, and for middle-class occupations vocationally-related education has either been optional (e.g. until recently lawyers and accountants were not required to have degree qualifications), or broad (e.g. medicine). Vocationalization therefore takes on a very different meaning in higher education (the growth of business studies and information technology programmes) from that in courses for sixteen-year-old school leavers, where the emphasis is on work experience, 'employment skills' and computer literacy.

Attempts to change educational policy in Britain have also been influenced by the peculiar structure of power in English and Welsh education with its complex combination of tradition, inertia and local autonomy. It was this capability of the system to preclude any planned change at all that led to educational policies being initiated by the Department of Industry (the funding of computer hardware for schools) and the Department of Employment (through its agency the Manpower Services Commission) which initially sponsored pilot courses in schools and colleges and now controls

25 per cent of the further education college curriculum. Previously, colleges and schools, though substantially funded by central government through the Department of Education and Science, were subject to local government control on matters of curriculum.

Perhaps the most radical attempt to introduce industrial sources of funds into education and to enable employers to gain a more direct control over the curriculum is the recently-announced proposal for City Technology Colleges. This will by-pass local government and give the opportunity for industrial and commercial sponsors to set up schools with government funding entirely independent of *local* education authorities.

The policies
Educational policies since the mid-1970s reflect a concerted attempt to achieve an education system more geared to industrial needs. The shift in emphasis can be identified in changes in: 1. the political control of education; 2. the forms of assessment; 3. the pedagogy; 4. the ideological context within which educational institutions operate.

1. Political control
The clearest examples of changes in political control are the TVEI (Technical and Vocational Education Initiative) introduced in 1983, work-related NAFE (non-advanced further education) which began in 1985, and GRIST (Grant-related in-service training for teachers) which began in April 1987. All represent new opportunities for central government to fund vocationally-oriented priorities in education. TVEI began as a pilot scheme to fund special courses in secondary schools, which emphasized new technology, careers advice and work experience. The schools involved (by 1985 only 3 per cent of pupils aged 14) received money for new equipment and buildings, curriculum development costs, and extra staff. As many commentators have noted, the relatively large funds available (£46 million in the first year) at a time of overall cutbacks proved irresistible to an increasing number of local education authorities. It was the first systematic attempt by government to direct funds to its priorities. TVEI has since been generalized to become a national plan for all secondary schools, and the model of control has been extended to further education colleges, and the in-service education of teachers. Further education colleges are now required to submit proposals for 25 per cent of their expenditure within the guidelines laid down by the Manpower Services Commission for *work related* programmes. This is in effect a rationalization of existing practice, as previously a proportion of

college programmes were sponsored and funded by the Manpower Services Commission (in particular YTS). The third extension of control over curricula is through the GRIST scheme for funding the in-service education of teachers. Local education authorities are required to bid for funds within central government guidelines, which give priority to links with industry, economic awareness and training in new technology.

2. Assessment

Assessment has been seen by government as a crucial element in changing curricula; as one senior government official put it: 'If we can achieve things with the new 17-plus examination, that will give us an important lever to vocationalize the last years of public schooling' (Ranson, 1984).

The examination he was referring to was the CPVE (Certificate for Pre-Vocational Education) which had its first candidates in 1986. CPVE is a programme designed for those staying on at school after the school leaving age or going to college, but who are pursuing neither a specific vocational course nor further academic studies. It is specifically geared to 'preparation for work', with much emphasis on the students finding out about themselves, and developing employment-related skills.

It reflects a wider pattern of changes in which even the traditional academic examinations are being reformed to include an emphasis on practical skills and competences. Examining bodies which have traditionally been limited to further education and the assessment of craft and technician skills are being encouraged to approve courses in the schools. The most recent initiative is the creation of the NCVQ (National Council for Vocational Qualifications) which will provide a set of national criteria for voctional competence in all fields, and will quite explicitly include the assessment of work-based learning. The NCVQ is being encouraged to use these criteria to negotiate comparability with school examinations.

3. Pedagogy and curriculum

The introduction of CPVE is one example of a number of curriculum initiatives which have been called 'the new vocationalism' (Cohen, 1984). The term refers to the emergence of programmes which have rejected a 'subject content' definition of a syllabus (for example English, maths, science and history) in favour of a modular framework specifying particular learning outcomes and the mastery of particular skills related to various occupational groupings (e.g. production, services, retail). These programmes have also rejected the traditional assumptions of a transmission pedagogy in favour of group tasks and assignments. The question that is raised by analyses such as Cohen's is whether the programmes, despite their official aims to extend access to those who have been disaffected from conventional schooling, will do other than 'socialize' those who participate in them into accepting personal responsibility for their uncertain future employment.

4. The ideological context

The final aspect of recent changes in education I wish to mention is one of context. This primarily effects colleges of further and higher education, but if the City Technology Colleges designed for pupils between 11-18 are established to compete with the schools, the change in context will operate at the school level as well. It can be described as the 'commodification' of education; colleges are being required to see themselves as providers or sellers of education and training on the market — many are appointing marketing officers to publicize courses with employers, and in some cases are competing directly with private training agencies. Whether this official support for an enterprise culture among educational providers will, in practice, increase consumer choice and opportunities is a question I shall return to in the last section of this chapter.

Views of vocationalization

These are some of the major elements of a set of policies aiming to 'vocationalize' education. They have met with resistance, though not overtly, at every level, and teachers and sometimes institutions have attempted to make out of such policies something that they could believe in as 'educational'. However, demography and shortage of funds have made schools and colleges with falling admission numbers vulnerable to the new sources of funds and students. The changes have not gone unnoticed by researchers, and it is to a number of their publications that I now turn. Each of them (Gleeson, 1985; Green, 1986; and Ranson, 1984) sets the changes in the provision for post-compulsory education in the wider context of central governments' economic policies; the outcome according to these authors is the emergence of new forms of tripartite stratification in the 16-19 sector of education.

The first of the three 'parts' is the 10-20 per cent on the academic route to higher education. There is very little change in the provision for this group, though two outcomes of the vocationalizing policies may affect this. University entrance remains based on three specialised A-level examination passes, which are themselves dependent on the student having done a range of specialist subjects at O level (when he or she is sixteen). With the change to GCSE at 16-plus which is a substantially less content-based examination, it will be harder for students to reach existing A-level standards at eighteen.* Secondly, the priority given to expanding the number of higher education students in technology is already leading to suggestions for broadening university entrance. Whether this will lead to fewer or new forms of stratification is not clear.

The second 'technical' tier of post-16 students will be those on Business and Technician Education Council courses, and increasingly those who have been through TVEI in schools. The third tier, often called 'the new FE' or 'the new sixth form' depending on where they are located, will be students on 'prevocational' courses such as CPVE and YTS. Despite the rhetoric of progression, these programmes, it is argued, are so limited in content, to make it all but impossible for students to 'progress', except in some cases into low-level employment. As Broadfoot points out (1986), the Scottish example in adopting a unfied system at 16-plus, at least in theory offers more possibilities, though the resistance there to accepting the new Scottish National Certificate as a basis for entrance to higher education is very strong.

The way forward

It is my view that these accounts, which emphasize the rationalizing and stratifying processes at work, though highly illuminating, are over-rationalistic and therefore over-deterministic. They suggest too great a congruence between employer needs and government policy and do not give enough scope to the reinterpretation of policies by teachers (and their students). I want therefore to conclude this chapter by presenting a rather different account which tries to link the contradictions at the level of policy with how they may be expressed at the level of practice.

One of the most striking things about Britain in the last decade is its

---

*The Education Secretary Kenneth Baker announced on 25 February 1987 the setting up of an independent committee on GCE A-level examinations. Under the chairmanship of Dr Gordon Higginson, vice-chancellor of Southampton University, its terms of reference are to recommend the principles that should govern GCE A-level syllabuses and to set out a plan of action to give effect to these recommendations. The committee has been asked to report by Easter 1988 (DES press release 52/87, 25 February, 1987). University vice-chancellors are pressing for the introduction of a more broadly based sixth-form curriculum, a reduction in the number of A-level syllabuses and more stress on a common core for each subject (CVCP press information, 26 June 1987).

remarkable political stability at a time when the economy appears in a process of near terminal decline. Evidence of the ability of the political system to absorb persistently high levels of unemployment, declining personal security and deteriorating public services is paralleled by evidence of a degenerating economy, in particular its manufacturing sector. The government solution is to accelerate the privatization of public services, and to cajole the education system to produce more technologists through the pressures of competition. Colleges that cannot sell their 'goods' are, like private firms, threatened with closure or mergers. The NCVQ referred to earlier is expected to facilitate this process by encouraging more and cheaper training, as employers and individual employees become more aware of the choices open to them. One aspect of this 'market economy' philosophy of education that receives less attention is that, like its forerunners in the 19th century, it espouses a doctrine of equal opportunities. The changes in educational policy I have outlined are intended to put educational provision within the reach of those groups who have not been motivated by the existing academic system which has systematically disadvantaged them. In other words a government that sees the country's economic salvation in the multiplying of technologists and marketing executives, wants as many girl technologists and marketing executives from ethnic minorities as it can get. Hence 'breaking down unnecessary barriers' is the educational slogan of the moment.

These are no more than elements in a fast changing educational landscape. However they suggest at least an attempt to shift from a top-down bureaucratic system with limited access to anyone who is not an academic success at school to a more open kind of educational market based on giving priority, where possible, to the choices of individuals as consumers. The question is whether these moves to a more open, market-centred, system of education will lead to new opportunities or, as the authors referred to above imply, new forms of exclusion. The policies as I have already indicated emphasize access, progression and at least the rhetoric of openness 'to the community' though this is rarely specified. Officially, government policies claim to want to overcome the barriers facing young blacks, girls and those with disabilities (though the barriers of social class are rarely mentioned).

The assumptions underlying the new curricula, new modes of pedagogy, and assessment are complex. On the one hand, it is expected that they will 'socialize' young people; as a DES official said in an interview quoted by Ranson (1984), 'If we have a highly educated and idle population — we may possibly anticipate more serious social conflict . . . People must be educated once more to know their place.' On the other the stress on 'unnecessary barriers' suggests a hope that they will tap that small section of previously excluded groups that have been denied through the academic system rather than their own lack of ability. The economy, it is argued will benefit, and those left behind will be there on merit, a plausible scenario when associated with a high technology economy of the future that some claim will no longer need the paid labour of the majority.

The aim of the policies we have outlined is to increase the flexibility of the education system, make it more adaptable to economic needs, and more accessible at a variety of points of entry to potential students. It can be seen, then, as an attempt to articulate new needs and to mould them in particular directions. It underlies the new educational language of student-centred learning and negotiated curricula. Such a policy has its risks: it has to allow projects which take advantage of the rhetoric of overcoming barriers and have the potential of empowering students who would not have thought they had demands to make on the system. Such a space, in becoming a possibility for a larger group than the policy intended, will inevitably become a site of competing attempts to colonize it.

The outcome remains uncertain — vocationalizing the curriculum at a time in which economic policies seem unlikely to expand employment opportunities could well create aspirations that cannot be fulfilled. Such contradictions may become sources of political change based upon new demands and new social movements. Whether they do so is a political question likely to be influenced by much more than the policies considered in this chapter. However, such a politics will have to be much broader than the conventional debate between political parties at election times. It will require those of us who support comprehensive education to go beyond the increasingly sterile debates between the 'academic' and the 'vocational', to articulate not just new pedagogies and curricula, but a new vision of education that starts from the deep and popular need to relate learning to work, but not in the narrowly occupationalist terms that characterize so much of recent educational policy.

References

Broadfoot, P. (1986), 'Assessment policy and inequality: the United Kingdom experience', *British Journal of Sociology of Education*, Vol. 7, No. 2, pp.205-24.

Cohen, P. (1984), 'Against the new vocationalism', in I. Bates et al., *Schooling for the Dole? The new vocationalism*. London: Macmillan, pp.104-69.

Gleeson, D. (1985), 'Privatization of industry and the nationalization of youth', in R. Dale (ed.), *Education, Training and Employment: towards a new vocationalism?* Oxford: Pergamon Press, pp.57-72.

Green, A. (1986), 'The MSC and the three-tier structure of further education', in C. Benn and J. Fairley (eds.), *Challenging the MSC: on jobs, education and training.* London: Pluto Press, pp.99-122.

Ranson, S. (1984), 'Towards a tertiary tripartism: new codes of social control and the 17-plus', in P. Broadfoot (ed.), *Selection, Certification and Control.* Lewes: Falmer Press, pp.221-44.

Production and Progress

Bernard Barker

After years of acute tension, education has entered an apparently convergent phase. Diverse pressures for change have coalesced in a futuristic reform movement driven by micro-technology and new teaching methods. MSC curriculum initiatives (TVEI, TRIST) have confounded critics by proving less utilitarian than many existing options (e.g., motor vehicle maintenance, typing) for low achievers. Pre-vocational courses stress personal and social development rather than the three Rs; examinations (GCSE, CPVE) have discarded the literary, academic approach associated with O level. The current emphasis on profiles, orals, practicals and coursework echoes a thirty year radical critique. The image of Dr Rhodes Boyson as a mid-Victorian employer insisting on accurate spelling and a sound knowledge of Imperial measurements has faded.

Traditionalists like Caroline Cox still seem to be in opposition, unable to evoke a response from pupils and teachers who have learned a new language. Pupils are autonomous; teachers are enablers. Assignments must be relevant and negotiated; practical, process skills must be developed through independent learning. Courses are exploratory and modular; assessments should record positive achievement. The vocabulary of in-service training and public debate suggests the child-centred world of A.S. Neill or Lawrence Stenhouse. Academic knowledge and teaching are discounted as confining and undemocratic; reformers are anxious to penetrate the privacy of the classroom and achieve 'fundamental change' in method, content and style. Each new scheme (Active Tutorial Work, Records of Personal Achievement) is part of a grand design, a formula to promote personal success in a future unlimited by culture or circumstances.

★ ★ ★

MSC, DES and HMI have become uncritical sponsors of a vague but progressive-sounding programme. Everyone is agreed that teachers 'must change' but precise accounts of desirable classroom practice are rare. Intentions and objectives are expressed in general terms (e.g. 'learning by experience'), open to a variety of interpretations. Proposals are often bland, tautological descriptions of attitudes and procedures, suggesting the advantages of enquiry, diligence or numeracy. The consequences for the conduct of particular activities are not explained. It is, after all, difficult to define lessons for others to teach, once traditional devices like syllabuses and past papers have been renounced. It is as if a fashion designer were preoccupied with style, omitting references to fabric and material.

Some techniques (e.g. learning by heart, note-taking, clause analysis) are disparaged more for their unfashionable, 'academic' or 'traditional' associations than for intrinsic faults. Imagine, for example, an English teacher working with a class on the text of Wilfred Owen's 'Anthem for Doomed Youth'. What would he/she make of the new approach? An English department familiar with current publications and anxious to share in the school's bid for TVEI funding might decide not to include poetry at all. Is verse relevant to industry or economic success? How many pupils are likely to be caught up in trench warfare? The study of language is perhaps unsuitable for those not destined for the higher ranks of the Civil Service. Or can Owen be justified as developing communication skills in a vocational setting (the army)? Literature might be admitted as an optional module.

The teacher has then to decide whether to supply an historical background or send pupils to view BBC 'Great War' videos. Textual exegesis is a plainly unacceptable procedure; youngsters' social and personal development would be better served by interviews with Somme veterans in a neighbouring old people's home. When the students begin to discuss the poem, however, difficulties multiply. The meaning of 'What passing-bells for these who die as cattle?' is not easily deduced from the words themselves. Language can depend on less than self-evident connections. Students may not recognize the alliteration of 'stuttering rifles' rapid rattle' or the pun of 'pallor' and 'pall' in 'The pallor of girls' brows shall be their pall'. Or are figures of speech intrinsically academic and irrelevant? What use is synecdoche in the modern world?

Terms like 'practical' or participatory' imply approval of craft or creative activities but such value judgements are unhelpful to students approaching a text. Does the phrase 'practical criticism' mean no more than careful reading and class discussion? Or should teenagers be left to discover rhythms and metaphors unaided? Is active experiment with a limited personal vocabulary preferable to the study of other authors? A teacher primarily concerned with texts might argue that without a critical training pupils may be incapable of independent judgements; that youngsters who learn to be as precise as Owen ('hasty orisons', 'shrill demented choirs') may avoid the vacuous generalities of modern thought.

Arguments for change and reform depend upon an unlikely stereotype of traditional practice. Few English staff, whatever their supposed style, aim to stifle discussion; fewer still devote their time to biography and history. Where are the advocates of content without understanding? The quality of a lesson depends in reality upon the knowledge, skill and education of the teacher, not his or her ideological orientation. Poetry teaching can be improved by courses in criticism or wide reading, not by a training in pedagogy which omits the material to be studied or communicated. An over-reliance on dictated notes is unlikely to be philosophical in origin. Overcrowded classrooms, examination requirements, shortages of books and a simple lack of imagination compel teachers to adopt strategies none would approve in theory.

★   ★   ★

The survival and success of the reform movement — in conditions apparently better suited to a traditionalist revival — derive in part from its vague optimism. 'Pre-vocational education' is an amorphous concept designed to satisfy CBI demands for an 'awareness of industry', parents anxious for modern equipment (word-processors, computers) and teachers attracted by a possible solution to the intractable problem of low attainment. Records of Achievement and Active Tutorial Work shift attention from depressing failure (content, examination results) to success (personal qualities, attitudes). GCSE is supposed to identify positive performance; a new statistical hyperbola (grade related criteria) seems to have replaced the depressingly normal distribution curve. TVEI has provided cash and a career structure when funds are short and promotion scarce.

Trojans like Holt (1982) criticize these Greek gifts as too useful, but are disarmed by the siren voices of progress. TVEI, for example, claims to encourage investigation, design and problem-solving. Those who question what is proposed or discover paradox rather than magic appear as disgruntled opponents of necessary reform. Since James Callaghan's Ruskin College Speech (in October 1976) politicians and employers have complained that schools do not produce a sufficiently skilled workforce for an advanced society. Comprehensives cannot be defended on their merits; pressures for educational change draw strength from wider social and political considerations. Corelli Barnett blames an academic bias in education and the Civil Service for Britain's relative decline in the twentieth century (Barnett, 1979). He argues that since the eighteenth century industry has been neglected in favour of an arcadian country life peopled by scholars and aesthetes. Japan and Germany are supposed to owe their economic successes to an emphasis on technological education and training.

Educational investment in the 1960s and 1970s failed to sustain Harold Wilson's 'white heat of the technological revolution' (see Foot, 1968, pp.150-4); schools and universities preferred to produce poets, merchant bankers and journalists. Such reasoning creates polarized generalizations beyond the scope of empirical investigation. Are science and culture necessarily incompatible? Can theory and practice be separated? Are music and drama less economically productive than manufacturing? The common-sense appeal of the utilitarian case is unaffected, however, by lack of evidence. Britain has fallen behind because she does not produce enough; if schools were to foster applied science, technology and design, output would increase. Relevant, practical, productive activities should be stressed; expressive or creative arts are alleged to depend on the success of manufacturing industry.

Production and growth are sacred, no longer subject to political debate. The TUC and CBI are committed to training and productivity; both support the elaborate structures of YTS and MSC. Young people are seen as objects to be prepared for 'the world of work'. Anti-industrial, even anti-capitalist, talk in the schools has become the scapegoat for the startling increase in youth unemployment since 1979. Productionists analyze social attitudes; they are unconcerned about the exchange rate or demand management. Psychological rather than political solutions are offered. Reform must be applied to the behaviour of individual teachers and pupils, not laws or institutions.

★　　★　　★

Schools operated on these commercial principles long before Shirley Williams' Green Paper (DES, 1977). Samuel Smiles' *Self-Help* (1859) encouraged Victorian people to consider their own character and conduct as a key to economic success. Teachers since have persistently urged children to link education with jobs and careers; examinations and qualifications are seen to play an important role in differentiating the labour force. Schools celebrate output and endeavour in equal measure, distinguishing pupils according to their pace of work and asking youngsters to fill as many exercise books as possible. Job-related considerations are introduced from the age of thirteen, when options are selected. Advanced level examinations are so difficult that most students are obliged to leave at the age of sixteen. British schools are in fact too concerned with short-term employment prospects; some of our present difficulties stem from premature vocational decisions rather than an academic disdain for industry. The clamour for 'change' is to some extent a call for more of the same, unsuccessful materialist approach. The vocational emphasis of the secondary modern in the 1950s did not lead to economic vitality or earn public esteem. Many apprentices trained in those days (as carpenters or metal workers) are unemployed now. City Technology Colleges are not an innovation but a repetition of a dismal experience.

'Productionism' is not a narrow doctrine, however. Despite the rhetoric of the Black Papers of the late 1960s and early 1970s, modern service-oriented industry seeks useful people rather than useful knowledge which is soon out-dated. An increase in social science graduates in the 1960s was supposed to create a managerial cadre; DES and MSC policy today is to spread a parallel technological consciousness throughout the population. The DES has argued consistently that the basic aim of education is 'to equip young people fully for adult and working life in a world which is changing very rapidly indeed in consequence of new technological developments'. The new utilitarians (following Barnett's thesis) are anxious to modernize and reform, not to foster a revival in traditional methods and scholarship. The aim is a change in social attitudes, not better spelling or arithmetic.

O'Hear identifies the irony of a Tory Government pursuing these white-coated dreams:

> The irony is that it is a self-styled Conservative administration which is vigorously pursuing policies in education which are the educational equivalent of the tower blocks and town centre 'developments' of the 1960s . . . utilitarian thinking and practice in education seeks to produce a population ready only to fulfil technological functions in society, their minds being left to their own weightless and autonomous choices among the stimuli produced by that technology and the mass media . . . . education for utility and education for autonomy are not necessarily antithetical (O'Hear, 1986).

A renewed emphasis on tradition, subjects, content and authority might indeed prove subversive of the Government's intentions. The education establishment, on its guard against the 'back to basics' movement, has been deceived by the new utilitarian strategy, recognizing only progressive virtue in schemes devised to create adaptable but obedient workers. TVEI and CPVE, in particular, set out to encourage qualities of character and personality; to develop transferable skills; to liberate young people from the unattractive features of mass culture (trade unions, restrictive practices, class solidarity) through dazzling silicone opportunities.

Robert Owen, mill-owner, educational reformer and socialist hero is an early example of the convergence of vocational and progressive purposes. As early as 1813 he wrote,

These plans must be devised to train children from their earliest infancy in good habits of every description . . . they must afterwards be rationally educated, and their labour be usefully directed (Gatrell, 1969, p.106).

Like modern TVEI co-ordinators, Robert Owen gave education a moral but practical purpose. People were to be rescued from dull, awkward ignorance and trained to conform to the requirements of the factory system. Goodness and usefulness are confused to the advantage of capital, which prescribes the future and determines the consciousness of labour. Progressive and vocational arguments tend towards a similar instrumental approach because neither really believe in education for its own sake. Disinterested scholarship cannot be trusted to promote either increased production or (for example) the liberation of ethnic minorities. Those influenced by progressive thought are inclined to think of learning as a method, an instrument to achieve change at a personal, individual level. Preoccupied by liberal principles, few remember that human rights and status cannot be improved without a changed conception of society. Increased output, wealth and consumption do not, in themselves, confer dignity.

*   *   *

The desire for a more equal, more competitive or more enlightened society is understandable but a poor foundation for an educational programme. Lessons, like Wilfred Owen's poem, have incalculable consequences, some spread over many years. A child may hear and enjoy the sound of a line ('in their eyes/Shall shine the holy glimmers of goodbyes'); understanding may be delayed until the reader reaches emotional maturity. Some may never glimpse the 'candles . . . held to speed them all?' or notice 'a drawing down of blinds'. Did the 'Anthem' 'do' for patriotism in inter-war Britain? Can sad songs make men happy? Who can say in advance which activities, experiences or methods may dispose people to be wise, virtuous, industrious or successful?

Late-nineteenth and early-twentieth-century reformers shared Rousseau's opinion that reason is on the side of the angels. Sidney and Beatrice Webb encouraged radicals to believe that the impartial accumulation of facts would lead to irresistible conclusions for policy and morals. Contemporary ideologues (of various persuasions) reflect disillusionment with this point of view and a mounting impatience with human beings. Policy statements indicating precise goals and objectives for education threaten to substitute the pursuit of intangible social outcomes for an objective curriculum. Teaching methods which mime the behaviour it is desired to reproduce can degenerate into moral propaganda of the Sunday School variety. Progressives and utilitarians are attracted, nevertheless, by similar taxonomies of educational objectives, purporting to identify desirable behaviour and activities for their achievement.

This is a forlorn enterprise based on a muddle. How can a causal link be established between particular factors influencing a child's development (e.g. home background, teaching methods, class sizes, single sex schools, curriculum patterns, mixed ability/setting) and alleged social and moral results? Statistical and survey techniques cannot provide consistent, valid, reliable indicators linking school 'improvement' or pupil performance with specific changes in methodology or curriculum. Ill-defined methods (e.g. 'problem-solving') seem to chase vague objectives (e.g. 'self-confidence') through nebulous subjects (e.g. 'social and environmental studies'). How can one strategy be recommended in preference to another if specified policy changes cannot be shown to lead to particular results (e.g. 'better schools', increased 'independence')? Ideologues in effect use homeopathic methods to reproduce and validate their own subjective social experiences.

*   *   *

A radical alternative to the 'production' model depends on rescuing certain insights from an absorbing entanglement with the vocational movement. The progressive tradition offers a series of profound observations about learning and human development which have been distorted and parodied in the contemporary obsession with useful change. The most important of these is a vision of the child as the subject of his or her own education. All real learning begins from the student's interests, concerns and preoccupations. Knowledge and language are not autonomous and independent, an objective reality unchanged by the activity of the learner. They are, rather, instruments through which the world may be understood and reconstructed; modes of symbolic representation through which a continuing dialogue may be sustained. Pupils search for means to express their emerging picture of the world, converting systems of thought and knowledge to serve new purposes. Each child has a unique, personal point of departure; he/she begins with an individual set of experiences, moving forward to encompass new territory and to build new networks. Youngsters progress through their own activity, in constant dialogue with people, culture, events and tradition. This description enables teachers to set helpful questions, encouraging natural instincts and approaches. The items below illustrate how teaching methods are suggested by a progressive view of learning:

Make a nailbox according to the following instructions *becomes*
Design a bridge with the maximum span possible using eight pieces of wood

Describe the steps by which Britain found herself at war with Germany in 1939 *becomes*
If you were Winston Churchill how would you respond to Hitler's peace offer and why?

Copy the sketch of a locust into your book *becomes*
What suggestions have you for controlling locusts?

In what conditions does barley grow best? *becomes*
If you were the farmer where would you plant the barley? (Barker, 1986, pp.112-13).

These questions try to make abstract ideas and information more accessible and tangible. Students are encouraged to make decisions as if they were involved; to imagine themselves as Churchill or a farmer. The principle can be extended to bring alive a wide range of subjects, enabling youngsters to identify with and work upon previously remote problems expressed in complex language. Progressive thought recognizes the need for a child to establish 'ownership' of an issue through a process of open enquiry. Consider the following example:

You are living in Florence in 1308. There are 300 cloth manufacturing firms in the town, and 30,000 skilled and unskilled workers dependent on the business. There is a 10 per cent fall in the price of raw wool in Europe.

1. Imagine you are a businessman. Explain your decisions on the

following points:

(i)   Whether you will need to reduce your prices on finished cloth this year.

(ii) Will you increase or reduce wages?

(iii) Will you employ more, less or the same number of craftsmen?

(iv) Will you increase or reduce output?

Remember, you will need to guess the likely outcome of other merchants' policies before you can work out your own.

2. Imagine you are are a weaver. Explain which of the following actions you will be prepared to take. Will you be successful?

(i)   Demand higher wages.

(ii) Go on strike.

(iii) Work longer hours.

(iv) Accept unemployment.

In each case, explain the reasons behind your decisions, e.g. as the raw material is cheaper, you may be able to increase output. If everyone does the same thing, there will be a surplus of finished cloth and cut throat competition cutting prices (Barker, 1976, pp.9-10).

Medieval economic history becomes a sequence of decisions for the pupil-businessman; a difficult, abstruse subject is converted into alternatives that can be discussed, assessed and decided upon. Young people can work together in groups, helping one another consider options; the teacher can explain points of difficulty. As solutions are pieced together, groups will form ideas about the wool trade; the activity is self-evidently more rewarding than taking notes from a book or chronicling events in a descriptive narrative. The assignment is not intended to manipulate the child or to promote a check-list of educational objectives. The purpose is, rather, to select the most interesting, rewarding and 'natural' approach to a topic chosen on its own merits.

These exercises start from a child's eye view of the world but are not simply circles drawn around a pupil's present interests. Questions aim to prompt a disciplined dialogue, a movement from the concrete to the abstract, from the particular to the general. Youngsters are free to experiment but are progressively engaged by a range of issues beyond the local context. Students' minds are not left 'to their own weightless and autonomous choices' but their creative, expressive instincts are focused on topics and problems outside themselves. Some attempts at progressive teaching (and most objections to progressive ideas) are based on a caricature in which children behave like adult artists and novelists, inspired, Fauve-like creature pouring forth an inner stream of consciousness in the modern style. Such images have not assisted the development of effective classroom teaching.

★ ★ ★

The limited aims outlined above would not satisfy the modern movement. Ideologues believe the power of new methods (found, for example, in Schools Council History or Nuffield Science) can be applied to achieve social, moral or economic objectives. MSC representatives would at once see the possibilities of *Florence 1308.* Here is a business simulation excellent for fostering 'young enterprise', relevant to industry and a contribution to economic awareness. Pupils will develop a range of skills useful in any employee, including deductive reasoning, analysis, numeracy and communication skills. The assignment could be described quite simply as a problem-solving exercise designed to educate for competence and capability. Attitudes vital for success in a technological society are also encouraged (e.g. flexibility, independence, toughness and curiosity). Only the Medieval connotations are unfortunate, introducing an irrelevant historical atmosphere and unnecessarily confusing the economic lessons to be learned.

A similar approach is adopted to experiments in Nuffield Science. Process-skills like observation, analysis, problem-solving and hypothesis formation displace natural phenomena as foci for lesson planning. Nothing can be studied for its own interest and value; no child can be left to explore, discovering unsuspected meaning and significance as the journey progresses. Instead there is a powerful, almost religious sense of purpose; children are set to unfold the providential workings of the world. Every possible educational benefit is tabulated; assessments are devised to ensure that the original prospectus of objectives has been realized and that each activity contributes to its declared goal. The prime objective seems to be a generation of modern, hygienic, technocratic children immunized against their own culture and history. Every conclusion or inference is pre-programmed.

Social reform and change have almost replaced disinterested learning as the approved objective of the school system. O'Hear (1986) believes that the radical Left and the Government no longer 'care about transmitting a genuinely disinterested vision of the human world, as a necessary prelude to any worthwhile life or action'. He follows Matthew Arnold 'in seeing the best hope for a democracy as lying not in the pursuit of self-government for its own sake, but in the imparting to its citizens ideals of high feeling and fine culture'. An explicitly utilitarian approach is not, however, a necessary consequence of progressive ideas and techniques but a result of the amorphous, politicized 'reform' agenda which has established an all but irresistible momentum, for reasons discussed above.

★   ★   ★

Radicals should resist the temptation to campaign for didactic methods or a return to the grammar school curriculum of thirty years ago. A 'back to basics' or 'traditional' outlook belong to an earlier period when board schools and mechanics' institutes were expected to civilize the working classes and prepare them for 'useful toil'. Progressive education still offers teachers a selection of powerful ideas with which to promote learning in comprehensive schools. It is. rather, the separation of progressive ideas from real events and phenomena which has so greatly assisted the instrumental attitude and should be resisted at all costs.

Aims, purposes and skills cannot stand in isolation from concepts and knowledge or alone provide an adequate guide to the range of human experience. Familiar academic disciplines with their long traditions of disinterested scholarship and characteristic modes of enquiry provide a far more secure basis for the school curriculum. Subjects and topics should be studied because they are judged valuable, worthwhile and interesting, not because they may promote various skills or objectives. Almost any topic can accommodate numeracy, communications skills, empathy or virtue; sets of criteria or objectives are of little help in writing syllabuses. 'Empathy', for example, does not suggest a particular subject (Lear? Red Indians? Vivisection? Charles I?) but diverts energy from teaching into the construction of tangled cross-definitions.

A broad selection of subjects tackled inventively can give youngsters a reasonable opportunity to develop concepts and ideas; teachers should be trusted to teach without a preliminary clutter of self-evidently desirable objectives. The curriculum should be 'content-led'; subject matter should be selected for intrinsic reasons, not to satisfy fashionable assumptions about useful activities and desirable products. Methods should be devised to help children study, not to condition them for a hypothetical future. Locusts and bridges should be the centre of education, not social qualities or intellectual procedures. Students should read 'Anthem for Doomed Youth' as a poem, not as an exercise in a phrenological gymnasium. Progressive education, with its emphasis on children's own interests and natural development, can become the best defence against those who wish to replace citizens with enterprising helots. It is essential to insist that the main purpose of education is not economic but political; youngsters must learn for themselves how to play a part in a democratic society.

References

Barker, B. (1976), 'Florence 1308', in *The Wool Trade of Medieval Europe, 1200-1450,* Academic and Business Mongraphs.

_____ (1986), *Rescuing the Comprehensive Experience,* Milton Keynes: Open University Press.

Barnett, C. (1979), 'Technology, education and industrial and economic strength', *Journal of the Royal Society of Arts,* February.

DES (1977), *Education in Schools: A Consultative Document* (Green Paper), London: HMSO, Cmnd. 6869.

Foot, P. (1968), *The Politics of Harold Wilson.* Harmondsworth: Penguin Special.

Gatrell, V. (ed.) (1969), *A New View of Society and Report to the County of Lanark* by Robert Owen (1813/21). Harmondsworth: Penguin.

Holt, M. (1982), 'The great education robbery', *The Times Educational Supplement,* 3 December.

O'Hear, A. (1986), 'Education beyond present desire', *Salisbury Review,* No. 4, 3 April.

Smiles, S. (1859), *Self-Help; with illustrations of character and conduct.* London: John Murray.

'Liberté, Egalité, Fraternité, ou la Mort': towards a new paradigm for the comprehensive school

Michael Fielding

'Liberté, Egalité, Fraternité, ou la Mort.' In the ambiguity of this aggressive greeting of French revolutionaries lies both the hopes and the demise of comprehensive education in this country. For revolutionaries of the 1790s the addition of 'ou la Mort' and the frequent production of a dagger to reinforce the point was a response to a situation in which cries of 'fraternity' were becoming mere mouthings by those whose sympathies lay elsewhere. However paradoxical such a greeting — expressed in even more heightened form in the 'politesse revolutionnaire' of 'Sois mon frere ou je te tue' ('Be my brother or I will kill you') — I find myself sympathetic with the predicament to which it was responding and wholly supportive of what I take to be the profound truth about the human condition to which it, perhaps unwittingly, gives expression.[1]

The predicament was one in which the bright hopes of the revolution were being undermined as the language of emancipation was being expropriated by the forces of reaction. It is arguable that a similar process of expropriation has gained headway in contemporary comprehensive education with the advent of the MSC and other government-inspired developments. Phrases like 'negotiated learning', 'active learning' and 'student-centred teaching' are no longer distinctive of 'progressive' education; and yet from the most right-wing Tory government since the Second World War it seems likely that what we are witnessing is more a form of linguistic subversion than the genuine embrace of the pedagogy of liberation. Similarly, the title 'comprehensive school' has come to mean a mere absence of selection at eleven, twelve or thirteen-plus rather than providing an indication of the values and educational practices which the institution embodies. The answer is not, of course, to produce real or metaphorical daggers at the throats of all who profess to be working in or supportive of comprehensive schools and demand that their practices match their rhetoric. As the demise of the 'tutoiement' of the early 1790s showed, not only is it impossible both theoretically and practically to impose fraternity, it is also less than reliable to treat the presence, or indeed the absence, of fraternal terminology as indicative of anything of much significance.

Yet we do need to do something. Writing some three decades after the beginning of the post-war campaign for comprehensive education, Hargreaves argued that: 'for many teachers and most parents there has simply been no explicit and clear rationale for the comprehensive school' (Hargreaves, 1982, p.78). Such an assertion should be a cause for concern. Champions of comprehensive education must, as Simon suggests, 'defend comprehensive schools' (Simon, 1986) — and you cannot defend something which amounts to little more than an umbrella term. The acid rain currently beating down on the public education system in this country is corrosive of more than the physical fabric of the institutions our children attend: the system itself is under attack and with it the democratic way of life which the trinome 'Liberté, Egalité, Fraternité' symbolizes. The additional 'ou la Mort' of my opening sentence takes on a new significance in Britain nearly two hundred years later. If we do not defend comprehensive schools successfully, if we do not unmask the pseudo-comprehensive discourse of Tory education policy, the gains which have been painfully won over decades will be undermined or reversed. Death is too final, too dramatic a term. But we should be in no doubt as to the nature and severity of the harm that will be done to the education of current and future generations and to our progress as a people towards a truly democratic way of life.

On the need for fraternity

If there are some important similarities between the predicaments facing those whose emancipatory aspirations foreshorten the two centuries which separate them, the vision which the exhortation 'Liberté, Egalité, Fraternité ou la Mort' enshrines seems to me at once more certainly and more profoundly true and as such it provides the key to a way forward, not only for comprehensive education but for our increasingly fragmented society. Consider two other nineteenth-century reflections expressed with equal conviction and in more positive a form:

Fellowship is life and lack of fellowship is death; and the deeds that you do upon the earth, it is for fellowship's sake that ye do them (Morris, 1886/7, p.51).

or

Only in community with others has each individual the means of cultivating his gifts in all directions; only in the community therefore, is personal freedom possible (Marx and Engels, 1845/46, p.83).

In the twentieth century its most compelling formulation came a further hundred years later:

> The democractic slogan — liberty, equality, fraternity — embodies correctly the principles of human fellowship. To achieve freedom and equality is to create friendship, to constitute community between men . . . (The) forces which unite men in fellowship express the ultimate nature of humanity. We can say that we enter into fellowship because that is our nature; that if we did not we should not be human; that if mankind was not united in this way there would be no mankind (Macmurrary, 1950, pp.74-5, 77).[2]

Within the last decade there has been a growing awareness of the truths towards which these insights point. Two of their most explicit proponents are sociologists, both of whom not only have the breadth of vision to realize the importance of an historical perspective in addressing our present needs, but are also thinkers deeply concerned with the education system as an important element in the creation of our current dilemmas and as a possible agent in their resolution. In his 1978 Reith Lectures, Halsey argued that:

> What is most clearly evident from the British experience, in my opinion, is an unresolved problem of fraternity or basis for social order beneath the clash of egalitarian and libertarian argument . . . Liberty and equality can operate as social principles only within the bounds set by fraternity . . . The way forward for Britain is to take its own traditions of citizenship and democracy seriously in all their richness and inspiration. They offer the basis for a new fraternity without which both liberty and equality are impoverished . . . We should seek fraternity as citizenship in all public organizations (Halsey, 1981, pp.10, 12, 162, 166).

An important means of nurturing that fraternal base is, Halsey suggests, a reformed educational system:

> an educational system giving balanced expression to the ideal of liberty and equality (which) would be a practical further development of the slow reform of the class-divided schooling bequeathed to Britain from liberal capitalism in the nineteenth century. The comprehensive primary and secondary school is its fraternal foundation, and could be the nursery of a fully democratic citizenship (ibid. p.167).

Some six years later, in a widely-read, exhilarating book by another Oxford sociologist, similar concerns provide the focus of the argument:

> (For Durkheim) true dignity and morality have a social and a corporate aspect. Genuine individuality must be rooted in group life . . . and group life was not

merely a means of giving people the social skills of co-operation and empathy, but of generating solidarity (which is the means of human fulfilment) . . . (The) solidary base of modern man could not be realized unless the spirit of association was already aroused . . . It (is) the school's key function . . . to 'breathe life into the spirit of association' (Hargreaves, 1982, p.111).

The extract is from the key chapter of Hargreaves's seminal *Challenge for the Comprehensive School*. The chapter itself ends with Hargreaves's advocacy that:

It is for us, in spite of the growth of individualism and the decline of community both in school and society since Durkheim's day, to find the means whereby that challenge (to provide the solidary base of modern man through nurturing the spirit of association) can be met in the new comprehensive schools of our own age (ibid. p.112).

This is the real 'challenge for the comprehensive school'; it is this linking of the demise of contemporary European society with the conditions of human fulfilment that make Hargreave's suggestions at once valid and challenging. At present there is scant evidence that the challenge has been even adequately understood, let alone seriously taken up. My own belief is that the strengths of the comprehensive school movement can fruitfully be understood only by evaluating the extent to which liberty, equality and fraternity have informed its history thus far; that a way forward emerges from an understanding of the relation between these principles; and that of the three, the last is, although the most neglected and least understood, the most important of all.

From equality of opportunity to equal value

The history of the fight for and gradual emergence of comprehensive schools as the main agent in the provision of comprehensive education is in some important respects similar to the struggle for democracy in European civilization. Whilst the political aspect of democracy has the earlier roots in time, until the seventeenth century it remained a largely negative concept with groups of one sort or another protesting their exclusion from a share of power. Summarizing and reflecting on this process Laski remarks that: 'The basis of democratic development is the demand for equality, the demand that the system of power be erected on the similarities and not the differences between men' (Laski, 1937, p.76).

Two aspects of these observations are relevant here. First the emergence of the aspirations of those fighting for democracy and those fighting for comprehensive education were at once reactive and emancipatory: for both the fight against perceived injustices provided the catalyst for their growth. The fight for comprehensive schools grew out of the experience of teachers, children and parents at the hands of a tripartite system which not only failed huge numbers of young people both personally and educationally but also rested on a psychological theory (to do with IQ testing) which turned out to be manifestly false. Ironically it failed to deliver the goods from the very meritocratic standpoint from which many current advocates of the return to the grammar schools now argue. The morass of problems endemic in the IQ testing scenario was exacerbated by the lack of sufficient movement between grammar, technical and secondary modern schools which the system, by its own admission, required. In their early days comprehensive schools appeared to address this problem successfully. When I first went to Thomas Bennett School in Crawley there were still a number of staff who remembered Tim McMullen, the first head, proclaiming the case of a girl who had gone from the thirteenth to the top stream and ended up at Oxford. Doubtless other pioneer comprehensives could tell the same tale. The exemplar illustrated the strength of the case for equality of opportunity which provided the political context for the early growth of the comprehensive schools, which more often than not intended to outdo the grammar schools. This last phrase is important because it indicates the strengths and the weaknesses of the early comprehensives: the strengths lay in their capacity to succeed in providing academic success for larger numbers of students, many of whom would have 'failed' in the tripartite system; the failure lay in their inability to recognize the inappropriateness of equality of opportunity as the guiding principle for comprehensive education.

Although Tim McMullen changed his views and his school and went on to be the first head of Countesthorpe College in Leicestershire, Thomas Bennett still made the qualitative leap from the reactive to the positive phase of comprehensive schooling. This was hardly surprising since the incoming head, Pat Daunt, can legitimately be regarded as one of the outstanding intellectual advocates of the comprehensive movement in the early 1970s. It is his book, *Comprehensive Values* (1975), that contains the clearest exposition of the principle of equal value which gave philosophical strength and form to a movement which was beginning to recognize the inappropriateness and straightforward impossibility of equality of opportunity. It is impossible because even if the starting line is uniform the arrival of the competitors in various states of fitness points to a race which has already been run in quite unequal circumstances. It is inappropriate because the imagery of races, competitors and inevitably few winners posits a meritocratic mode of life in which the success of a very small number in a narrow field is predicated on the failure of vast numbers of their fellow citizens. It is sharply out of tune with a view of society which seeks to value all its members in all their diversity.

Since the mid-1970s the advance of comprehensive schooling has slowly passed through its reactive phase and is now substantially into the phase of advocacy. Hargreaves was over severe in stating that: 'Today we know what the comprehensive schools were designed to be *against*. Until we ask ourselves what comprehensives are *for* they cannot go beyond the meritocratic principles on which at present they somewhat uneasily rest', Hargreaves, 1982, p.74). He seemed curiously unaware that his *Challenge for the Comprehensive School* formed part of a debate that Daunt, Marsden and others had started more than a decade earlier. That uncharacteristic historical lacuna does not, however, detract from the importance of his contribution. In many respects the phase of advocacy is the most difficult time thus far in the history of the fight for comprehensive education. The injustices and iniquities of the old tripartite system have taken on new, less immediately obvious forms and many of those issues which need to be addressed find their reference points within the comprehensive schools themselves. Hargreaves' book was more that just another publication from an academic. It was, by its own admission, 'directed to the . . . audience of practising teachers rather than to academic colleagues' (ibid. p.x) and its impact on the debate about the nature of specifically comprehensive education was considerable. He reaffirmed the necessity of the comprehensive school going 'beyond meritocracy', gave further practical force to the 'equal value' principle by highlighting the importance of human dignity and its implications for the outmoded cognitive-academic curriculum, and gave further impetus to the comprehensive community school movement.

Above all, Hargreaves sought not just to reflect on and extend the commitment to the equal value principle and its practical outcomes in terms of the curriculum and the dynamic role of the community school; the overriding 'challenge for the comprehensive school' turned out to be even more deeply rooted. It amounted to something like a paradigm shift from an individualistic notion of education (exemplified by the 'fallacy of individualism') to one which is communitarian, which starts by asking questions about the kind of society we wish to live in and the role of education in its realization, and regards individual flourishing as inextricably communal. At root the communitarian paradigm grows out of a different social and political tradition, which argues that the atomistic model of human beings on which so much of our contemporary educational and social practice rests is deeply misconceived; which instead argues that: 'It is only in relation to others that we exist as persons . . . This mutuality provides the primary condition of our freedom' (Macmurray, 1961, p.213).

The rejection of individualism

A shift in modes of though and feeling which helps us to establish an alternative educational paradigm is not, of course, an easy matter. It is not, however, an insuperable task. There is a tradition of social, educational and political thought which Hargreaves and Halsey both draw on and contribute to. That tradition needs to be rediscovered and nurtured. In it we shall find pointers to practice and a richness of inspiration which will enable us to respond with more confidence to what we are once again beginning to feel, but which the contemporary educational hegemony denies. Milan Kundera's reminder that 'The struggle of man against tyranny is the struggle of memory against forgetting' is particularly apt in a society in which the popular memory is too often circumscribed by the media manipulations of a conspicuous present and the partiality of privilege which, for example, cherishes the clarion call for the return to grammar schools on the tacit assumption that one's own children will not find their way into the local secondary modern school.

The values to which our experience begin to point more insistently bring us back once more to Laski's stress in his history of democracy on 'the similarities and not the differences between men' (Laski, 1937, p.76). They enable us, too, to appreciate the importance of Halsey's observations that:

> We still have to provide a common experience of citizenship in childhood and old age, in work and play, and in health and sickness. We have still, in short, to develop a common culture to replace the divided cultures of class and status (Halsey, 1981, p.164).

The driving force of some of the developments in comprehensive schools in the last two or three decades, such as the move towards the common core curriculum, have been fired in part by recognition of this very need. There are signs, too, that Halsey's call for the comprehensive primary and secondary school to provide the 'fraternal foundation' of a reformed education system and take on the role of 'the nursery of a fully democratic citizenship' is being heeded. Bernard Barker's *Rescuing the Comprehensive Experience* has as its final chapter heading 'Towards the common school?'

The concluding section of the chapter is headed 'Citizenship' and in it Barker argues strongly that: 'Schools could become influential in developing a revival in citizenship and self-government' (1986, pp.148-9).

The significance of Barker's book goes beyond this commitment to the importance of citizenship. It fruitfully examines the case for alternative management styles and a more active pedagogy from a perspective broadly in tune with the communitarian tradition which I am suggesting provides the most appropriate framework for the new comprehensive paradigm. The broad delineation of that paradigm and some brief reflections on a number of developments which lead me to offer it as a possible way forward comprise the final two sections of this chaper.

The fraternal alternative

What, then, are the broad characteristics of the paradigm I am suggesting as appropriate for the development of comprehensive schools over the next decade? The fundamental principles on which it rests are those of the democratic movement itself, best summed up by the French trinome of Liberty, Equality and Fraternity. At first glance, they seem vague and only obscurely connected with an undertaking as severely practical as the daily experience of schooling and education for young people. But their power rests firstly in the unfailing persistence with which many draw inspiration and moral legitimacy from their invocation; secondly it rests on their interconnectedness. Indeed, it is interconnectedness which give them their emancipatory potential. Each on its own is only contingently related to democracy and the excesses of each uninformed by the significant presence of the others may lead, for example, to a freedom which favours only those with wealth and power, to an equality which mistakes uniformity for fulfilment, or to a fraternity whose boundaries are narrowly drawn round the disfigured template of fascism.

As a way into understanding and exploring the potency of the new paradigm it might be helpful, at least in the first instance, to look at ways in which some of the undoubted achievements of the comprehensive movement can be adequately described and evaluated through the extent to which they have been informed by commitment to the principles of liberty, equality and fraternity.

Curriculum development — liberty or equality?

One of the areas on which current debate is focusing most intensely is the curriculum. In the 1960s and early 1970s the concern was largely for freedom, particularly in the large schools where it became a matter of pride that the number of subjects on offer could without falsification be reckoned in multiples of ten. The '57 Varieties' curriculum initially held attractions, but in many schools it became clear that the choices were more apparent than real and that status differences between the formal possibilities reinforced negative attitudes and did not provide the motivational impetus intended. The freedom of such choice turned out not to be liberating, at least not for eighty per cent of those who had theoretical access to it.

A more fruitful response to the libertarian impulse was the growth and development of Mode 3 courses at both CSE and O level. Here the choices were available within subject areas and what was on offer was intended to be more in tune with the needs of the students for whom the course was created. At their best such syllabuses not only offered students the opportunity of choosing from a menu compatible with their own cultural and communal context; it also offered opportunites for them to create parts of the course themselves, if you like, to do their own cooking. They were in some respects a forerunner of the negotiated learning currently available in CPVE and similar courses where again the freedom is made jointly available to student and teacher in the process of dialogue. Some schools such as Stantonbury Campus in Milton Keynes also sought to widen the scope of choice still further by schemes such as Day 10 and Week 10 in which the traditional school curriculum was enriched at regular intervals by staff, and to a lesser extent students and parents, offering a variety of sessions from Mexican cookery to mountaineering. The most recent feature of curriculum development expressing the principle of freedom is the modular curriculum in which for varying proportions of time students choose from a variety of short courses. By and large such modules are heavily teacher-dominated and the scope of choice lies between different offerings rather than providing relative autonomy within them.

Not all overt curriculum development has, of course, been in response to libertarian pressure. The '57 Varieties' model began to break down, not just because its surface features disguised a reality that for most students was no different from its more restricted forerunners, but also because the divisiveness and fragmentation of the ideology of equality of opportunity from which it was born was being challenged by those whose allegiance was more attracted to the creation of a common culture. The most positive outcome of this egalitarian thrust was the move towards integrated curriculum areas: English, while often still retaining the two exam titles English Language and English Literature, is nonetheless unitary in its conception and delivery; Integrated Humanities is increasingly replacing the separate courses in History, Geography and the Social Sciences; Integrated Science is no longer a 'lesser' alternative to the study of Physics, Chemistry and Biology; and integrated approaches in CDT and the Expressive Arts are being developed. What these developments enable us to do is to move much more firmly towards a common core curriculum which is potentially a powerful agent of a shared culutural experience within schools.

A complementary egalitarian challenge to curriculum development has come from those who wish to rid comprehensive schools of the cognitive-academic model which has dominated our thinking in secondary education for so long. The specifically egalitarian nature of the argument lies in its insistence on the importance of the dignity of all students and the corollary that we need to offer a curriculum appropriate to a comprehensive school and not a grammar school. The suggestion is not that we have a resuscitation of Bantock's advocacy of a separate curriculum for non-academic students or, in its current metamorphosis, a pre-vocational band of studies or something especially designed for low attainers. Rather it is the positive arguing for a curriculum which is supportive of the development of all aspects of our humanity, in particular those areas such as expressive arts and community studies which are rich in what Hargreaves, following Durkheim, calls 'solidary' experience.

Curriculum development — liberty, equality, fraternity

I am aware that this sketch is of neccessity incomplete: it does not cover the delivery of the curriculum which various structures enable or preclude; it says nothing about the hidden curriculum. Nonetheless, it does illustrate the way that curriculum developments in comprehensive schools have been influenced by the principles of liberty and equality. And it does begin to offer some grounds on which we might judge the wisdom or otherwise of the form those developments have taken in schools. My own view is that unless curriculum developments express both liberty and equality simultaneously, unless our social, educational and political relationships are informed by both principles, they cannot hope to help us towards a more democratic way of life. In specifically curricular terms, unless we can be sure that students are treated in such a way as to be manifestly of equal value and unless we ensure that they are accorded a freedom which demonstrates that we are fostering their agency as developing human beings, then we are failing to practice the ideals we espouse. Until now the curricular arrangements in comprehensive schools have tended to emphasize liberty at the expense of equality, or vice versa. Our way ahead must be informed by both — and by the third principle of fraternity without which neither can develop fully or even well.

The key features of fraternity and similar relations between human beings are firstly that they are caring relationships, not just for some aspect or part of someone, but for them as a person. They are personal, not functional, relationships. Secondly, they are characterized by liberty and equality. Fraternal relations cannot exist if these are absent; without liberty and equality their growth is temporary or distorted.

If my understanding of the conditions of human fulfilment is correct, application of this third principle of fraternity or community to education in general, and to curriculum development in particular, should enable us to begin to evaluate the strengths and weaknesses of our current position and seek emancipatory pointers for the future. What the fraternal principle does is basically two things. Firstly, since it is constituted by liberty and equality it forces us to look at current developments and ask ourselves whether both principles are sufficiently active. In an ideal world they would be, and, in a sense, there would be nothing else to do other than ensure their life and vigour for, as has been suggested earlier:

> The democratic slogan — liberty, equality, fraternity — embodies correctly the principles of human fellowship. To achieve freedom and equality is to create friendship, to constitute community between men (Macmurray, 1950, pp.74-5).

In the absence of that ideal we should, secondly, ask ourselves not only whether the reciprocally conditioning principles of liberty and equality are being pursued, but also whether the values embedded in our curriculum model, the practical structures which provide its organizational context, and the human relations that characterize its delivery are in tune, not only with one another but with the overarching concern with our development as persons in community. These questions bring us back very firmly to the human purposes of education. Fundamentally education is about helping each other to enrich our humanity, to become more fulfilled as persons and, given the nature of personhood, that can be done only in community, in relations in which we care for each other as persons.

An interesting example of current curriculum development to which these principles might be applied is the increasingly popular modular curriculum adopted by many in the vanguard of comprehensive education. Leaving aside the degree to which it accomodates a dynamic relationship between the principles of liberty and equality, to what extent does a modular curriculum enhance or rupture our capacity to retain a holistic sensitivity to each person's development? to what extent are relationships with young people affected so that diversification becomes, in the end, fragmentation? Advocates of different modular schemes will, of course, respond to these questions in different ways: the important thing is that the issues such questions raise are faced; in its fullest form the fraternal or communal imperative is the most effective guarantor of our human education. Certainly, some variants of the curriculum developments mapped out earlier pay no attention whatever to such considerations and any system which creates a significant gulf between 'pastoral' and 'academic' aspects of education severely compromises its creative potential.

The emancipatory imperative

The composite nature of the principle of fraternity ensures the emancipatory intent which has underpinned the comprehensive school. The comprehensive school movement has always been concerned with challenging orthodoxies; either by championing equality of opportunity and the erosion of privilege; or by the affirmation of the equal value principle and the rejection of meritocracy; or, currently, by the challenge to the individualist model of human fulfilment. The comprehensive school movement is the voice of a democratic, public education and, as such, it speaks for communities and ways of life that the grammar, secondary modern and public schools never could. The principle of fraternity is itself the interpersonal grounding which makes possible both public democratic polity and personal human fulfilment.

> Freedom is the product of human fellowship . . . Politics is necessary to freedom . . . But a democratic polity is possible only for a human community which has established a common way of life upon a basis of mutual trust; and the extent and quality of the freedom it provides depends upon the extent to which those it governs and organizes are in communion with one another (Macmurray, 1950, pp.104-5).

A new comprehensive paradigm

The challenges which lie ahead for the comprehensive school are the challenges that face us as persons in the different sorts of relations — social and political, personal and communal — which condition our destinies in the last decade of the twentieth century. For those of us whose direct concern is with the nature and quality of comprehensive education our most pressing need is to reject the contemporary managerialism and address ourselves again to purposes, to the basic question of what comprehensive education is for. Only when we have done that will the appropriate means at our disposal emerge. What is clear from the outset is that they will not be freewheeling techniques applicable to a multitude of purposes; they will be approaches informed by the values which are fundamental to our undertaking.

My own view is that we need an alternative paradigm of comprehensive schooling which has its roots in the communitarian tradition of social and political thought and that central to that paradigm is an emancipatory imperative. Of course, even if we were to develop our practices within that framework the way ahead would not be any less free from contention and disagreement. The authors of the quotations which form part of the opening section of this essay would certainly not agree on a number of issues of considerable importance for educators. What William Morris, Karl Marx and Friedrich Engels, John Macmurray, A. H. Halsey, Emile Durkheim and David Hargreaves would all agree on is not just the 'fallacy' of individualism but its destructiveness of human flourishing.[3]

In all this there is a problem of language. Ignatieff may well be pointing to something important when he says:

> Words like fraternity, belonging and community are so soaked with nostalgia and utopianism that they are nearly useless as guides to the real possibilities of solidarity in modern society . . . Our task is to find a language for our need for belonging which is not just a way of expressing nostalgia, fear and estrangement from modernity (Ignatieff, 1984, pp.138-9).

We need a language which is sensitive to the struggles of oppressed groups within our society. It might well be that words other than 'fraternity' or 'fellowship' become more appropriate to that task. Words which express deep human aspirations are often contested, always historically conditioned, yet fundamental to our growth as persons:

> We need words to keep us human . . . Without a language adequate to this moment we risk losing ourselves in resignation towards the portion of life which has been allotted to us (ibid. pp.141-2).

The importance of words lies ultimately in the reality which they seek to reflect and create. Near the beginning of William Morris's 'A Dream of John Ball' the narrator ponders on:

> how men fight and lose the battle, and the thing that they fought for comes about in spite of their defeat, and when it comes turns out not to be what they meant, and other men have to fight for what they meant under another name (Morris, 1886/87, p.53).

Our fight is for comprehensive schools because they are currently the most appropriate means to the education of all young people. The comprehensive ideal is by its very nature emancipatory and the principle of fraternity sets out the conditions of its success.

Some might argue that calls for fraternity are merely utopian at a time in which individualism is throttling the life out of an already emaciated public education system. Whilst we speak of unity and common purposes the current realities of our society have more to do with division, the partiality of privilege and the secular beatification of greed. Such arguments fail in the end to convince for at least two reasons. Firstly, how can supporters of comprehensive schools acquiesce in the destruction of the system they have fought to establish? Secondly, and more importantly, is it just utopianism to recognize that something needs to be done, and to go on to address more profound questions about the nature and conditions of human fulfilment? At the heart of the comprehensive ideal lies a belief about what it means to be and to become more fully human. The conditions that enhance our growth as persons are under attack, but the necessity of those conditions remains absolute. The necessity of loving our children does not diminish in proportion to increases in the hostility of the social and political world in which they grow up. Rather the reverse. Likewise in schools, the communal or fraternal imperative becomes more, not less, important as the prevailing climate becomes increasingly individualistic. Schools cannot win through on their own, but they cannot win at all if they do not enter the fight.

Acknowledgement
I should like to thank Graham Benjamin, Roger Dale, Patricia White and John Wilkins for comments on an earlier draft of this paper.

Notes
1. The use of the term 'fraternity' in this chaper is not gender-specific. I have retained its use throughout in order to maintain a linguistic thread which, if broken, might well lead to confusion in an already difficult area. It may well be that words other than 'fraternity' or 'fellowship' are more appropriate to the emancipatory task I am advocating.

2. John Macmurrary's writings on education are outstanding, but not readily available. Of particular interest are the papers: 'Learning to be human' (5 May, 1958); 'Teachers and pupils' (29 November, 1963); and 'Reflections on the notion of an educated man' (17 November, 1965). None of them were published. The author

of this chaper, who can be contacted at Stantonbury Campus, Milton Keynes, MK14 6BN, would be happy to make copies available to interested readers.

3. I realize, of course, that the term 'individualism' is itself subject to considerable debate. In his review article 'Durkheim's call to order', *New York Review of Books,* 7 March, 1974 (p.26), Alasdair MacIntyre argues that:

> the essence of individualism is not so much to emphasize the individual rather than the collective . . . as to frame all questions according to an ostensible antithesis between the individual and the collective.

Of the authors cited in this chapter, Macmurray is arguably the most compelling and the most eloquent in his rejection of individualism thus conceived. According to MacIntyre, despite an obvious hatred of individualism, Durkheim remained a victim of its distinctive mode of thought.

References

Barker, B. (1986), *Rescuing the Comprehensive Experience.* Milton Keynes: Open University Press.

Daunt, P. (1975), *Comprehensive Values.* London: Heinemann.

Halsey, A. H. (1981), *Change in British Society.* Oxford: Oxford University Press.

Hargreaves, D. (1982), *The Challenge for the Comprehensive School.* London: Routledge and Kegan Paul.

Ignatieff, M. (1984), *The Needs of Strangers.* London: Chatto and Windus.

Laski, H. (1937), 'Democracy', in E. Seligman, (ed.), *Selections from the Encyclopaedia of the Social Sciences.* New York: Macmillan.

Macmurray, J. (1950), *Conditions of Freedom.* London: Faber and Faber.

_____ (1961), *Persons in Relation.* London: Faber and Faber.

Marx, K, and Engels, F. (1845/46), *The German Ideology* (1970 edition). London: Lawrence and Wishart.

Morris, W. (1886/87), 'A Dream of John Ball' in *Three Works by William Morris* (1973 edition). London: Lawrence and Wishart.

Simon, B. (1986), *Defend Comprehensive School.* London: Communist Party of Great Britain, October.

Gender, Race and Class: essential issues for comprehensive education

Carol Adams

While issues of race and gender appear on the current educational agenda, there is little overall consensus as to their importance, position and permanence on that agenda. While they are given high priority in some local education authorities, they are still regarded by many people as peripheral issues rather than essential and at the very heart of education.

In this chapter I shall argue that gender, race and class issues are of central importance in any planning for the future of comprehensive education — that is, an education that meets the needs of all children. Those of us working in the field of equal opportunities must spell out the reasons for this with clarity and urgency.

It is important to understand how the comprehensive debate in the past attempted to take up concerns of class but often reinforced social differences through what it offered. The creation of mixed comprehensives gave support to the belief that equality would be achieved by mixing everyone up, and treating them all the same. In practice, girls and boys (and subsequently black and white pupils) were often directed towards a differentiated curriculum aimed at different vocational outcomes (e.g. Newsom, 1963). In current and future planning, concerns about class should not be lost but must be redefined along with those of race and gender. A secondary education system which is basically geared to the needs of white middle class boys continues to short change and fail the majority — female, black, working class. Our knowledge of the experience of these children demands urgent, radical change, not cosmetic or token gestures.

Pupils' experience of schools

Research on race and gender

There is no lack of evidence to show that secondary schools currently fail large numbers of children, including many who enter those schools with no record of underachievement in their primary school. Eccleston (1985) and Wright (1985), have demonstrated the failure of schools to meet the needs of black children, as illustrated through examination results and destinations after leaving school. 'These differences in examination performance do not necessarily reflect the abilities of the young people . . . If racial prejudice operates among teachers, low examination achievements could indicate even less adequately than usual the young person's occupational capacity'. (Eccleston). Wright found that pupils of West Indian origin with high attainment levels were allocated to the lower bands and that their representation in certain option groups such as physics was not clearly related to their exam results. 'Social reasons', or behaviour, were also taken into account when allocating these pupils to ability groups. This led to the 'cataclysmic decline in the relative position of these West Indian pupils during their five years of secondary education'.

While girls achieve overall more highly than boys in examination terms, they are grossly under represented in those subject areas which lead to the most sought after qualifications and better paid employment in the scientific and technological areas. Girls are often required to have higher marks in comparison to boys in order to study physics (Pratt, 1984; APU, 1986). Stanworth (1983), has shown how the achievement levels of girls can be underestimated and undervalued by the teachers, by male pupils and thus by the girls themselves in comparison to boys. It has been well documented that girls overall get less than their share of resources in terms of teacher time and attention in the classroom, as well as space around the school and access to equipment (Spender 1980; Delamont 1980).

However, this must be qualified by the evidence that black girls and boys often share common experiences as black pupils — for example, some black girls feel that they get more than their share of teacher attention, but, as with black boys, this is experienced as negative and punitive (Wright, 1987). Sharpe (1976) found that black girls were highly motivated to leave school with qualifications and worked hard to that end, in contrast to some white girls.

Thus at times black girls and boys share common experiences of school on account of their race; at other times black and white girls share common experiences based on gender; and at times the experience of being black and female in school will be different from that of being black and male or white and female. It is vital to be aware of how both forms of discrimination operate in order to broaden and deepen our understanding of inequality.

Connections with class

The third influence, harder to identify and quantify but just as powerful and closely bound up with pupils' race and sex, is that of class. Since most black pupils are from working-class backgrounds much of their experience, for example in terms of housing, employment or the lack of it, area of residence, is that of being working class with the added dimension of being black. The cultural background of working-class white boys has been studied for some time but only relatively recently has it been considered in terms of the influence of race (Willis, 1978). The ideology of femininity has tended to disguise the class differences between middle and working-class white girls (Arnot, 1983), until recently when studies of working-class girls' lives (McRobbie, 1978) have made visible the very different versions of feminine culture reproduced through class divisions. The experience of being working class might be as or more powerful for some pupils than that of being male or female.

Acknowledging the impact of class on black and white pupils' lives outside of school is essential for understanding their different responses to the 'culture' of school, essentially an elitist one which often reflects upon children's home backgrounds as inadequate, deprived or deviant. Class is the cement that binds together the experience of race and gender in pupils' lives. Looking at how all three influences operate leads away from the view that racism is about the 'problem' of black pupils in inner city schools or that sexism is about the treatment of girls in large mixed comprehensives.

In a wider analysis, we need to ask what have been the forces at work which lead to the absence of black pupils in some schools and some areas — e.g. social class origins, residential patterns, racism, cultural values, and similarly, the absence of black teachers. Race is an issue for all white schools, just as gender is an issue in all boys' and in all girls' schools. Rather than presenting class, gender and race as competing oppressions affecting different pupils in different schools we need to examine how all three factors work together.

Responses to equality issues

If the basic principle of comprehensive education is to be realized — the maximum achievement and fulfilment for all pupils, — then the history, experience and identity which each pupil brings with her/him into the classroom, located in her/his sex, race and class must be acknowledged and understood. This needs to be done with sensitivity towards the individual, avoiding the pitfalls of stereotyped assumptions about the characteristics of so-called 'ethnic groups' or working-class families. The more we are able to understand what pupils bring with them, the clearer it becomes that the 'individual child' who has been the 'norm' for Western educational thinking, has been a white middle-class male. Most of our pupils do not share his past background, present perceptions or future opportunities. and because of this may be seen as resistant, misfits, 'problem children', 'less able'. Many pupils will be limited through a range of restricted expectations from teachers, parents and themselves, mostly unconsciously and unintentionally, because they 'fail' in some way to meet the accepted 'norm'. From infancy children are conditioned to accept their role in an unequal society and although they also learn strategies of resistance and defiance, by the time of secondary school the influences of society's expectations will have had its impact on pupils' indentities.

Therefore the view of equal opportunities that 'We treat them all alike regardless of race, sex or class' is actually a block to any realistic steps towards equality. We have only to glance at educational history — the post-war provision of the tripartite system of secondary education for all, for example, to see that those who benefit most from the availability of opportunities to 'succeed' are those in the most favourable position to take up those opportunities — plus perhaps the very lucky few (Centre for Contemporary Cultural Studies, 1981). What is offered as opportunity to achieve and 'like' treatment can be highly unequal and differentiated in how it is perceived and received. So, for example, the opportunity to study for a career or to take up training in a traditionally male vocational area will be received differently by a middle-class girl, for whom the prospect may be in keeping with parental aspirations and the life styles of adult women she knows, and a working-class girl, for whom the prospect might be unfamiliar, alien and in direct conflict with the ideals of femininity on which homelife and peer group culture are built. As Isaacson (1986) has demonstrated, what might appear as freedom from a privileged perspective, for example to make certain subject choices, might not be perceived as such at all by black and white working-class girls for whom life might hold other priorities. Similarly, the incentive to study for future reward in the form of employment will be accepted or rejected depending on the situation pupils experience in their communities, among family and peers.

The offer of an equal education is, therefore, only meaningful if accompanied by positive action which takes into account pupils' relationship to the education system. The basis for such action must be understanding of young people themselves, still as individuals, but individuals who are black and/or female and working class and whose lives are very much affected by the realities of the world outside the classroom. This argument is only too familiar to those many teachers who are engaged in reflection and change towards making their teaching and their schools relevant and responsive to their pupils' needs. But the future of secondary schools is unlikely to be determined by the efforts of teachers who are committed to the realization of greater equality, and the centrality of gender, race and class issues in comprehensive education needs to be argued publicly and at all levels wherever policies for the future are determined.

The school structure

Why is it that schools are better able at the moment to respond to the needs of some pupils than of others? What do the structures of secondary schools represent in terms of race, sex and class differences? What are the underlying principles on which schools are organized?

A school's aims, traditions, what it openly seeks to promote and what is taken for granted will firstly influence the clientele attracted to the school, but will also affect the different groups of pupils which make up the school population. The population itself is significant in terms of class, race, single sex or mixed, and the balance or otherwise of the sexes. The curriculum on offer, including option choice and how it is organized, will have considerable implications for girls and boys, black and white as will the provision of facilities — lack of technical facilities and home studies facilities in girls' and boys' schools respectively being a notable example. The organization of students, into mixed ability groups, streams, sets or bands, can be highly significant in terms of race and class as well as of gender. Which groups of pupils take the so-called non-academic, vocational subjects? Who is eligible to take a second language? Does the overall curriculum of girls and boys, from different racial groups tend to be different? Which pupils receive learning support? How is the teaching of English as a Second Language organized?

Curriculum content is another obvious medium for upholding and transmitting particular sets of values. The traditional secondary curriculum, inherited from the grammar schools, emanated from the white, male, middle and upper-class world of the universities where there were, until relatively recently, no women or black people. How far the curriculum has been modified in the light of a redefinition of what is necessary, relevant and appropriate for secondary pupils in the 1980s, albeit within the limitations of examination syllabuses, available resources and teacher expertise, again varies enormously between schools. Do the materials used and resources displayed reflect the contributions to human knowledge of both women and men from a variety of cultural backgrounds, or is there a concentration on the traditional heritage of great white men from history, literature and world affairs?

The staffing of schools — women and men, black and white, teaching and support staff — and their positions in the structure are another indicator of what the school represents. Communications with parents and the ways in which parents are regarded by the school is another. Are 'one parent families' or 'Asian families' regarded as a problem and as homogenous groups? Another indicator is the pastoral system, the rules, rewards and punishments including exclusions and suspensions. Some groups of pupils are often over-represented as recipients of such measures. The occupation of space around the school — playground, corridors, classrooms, staircases — by different groups of pupils, often representing subcultures of the school, is often highly significant in terms of gender and race.

Some schools have produced written policies on racism and sexism and that represents a significant commitment at least in principle. However, it is the living policy, the behaviours, language and attitudes that are expressed daily by students and teachers that provides a more accurate indicator of the school's ethos and of how it will be experienced by different pupils.

It is important to consider the impact that the school structures and policies are likely to have on pupils' perception of the social world and their own ability to change it. The more controlled and powerless pupils feel, the less likely they are to feel that they are able to challenge stereotypes of sex and race. If pupils are encouraged by the learning system of the school to develop a sense of autonomy, to believe that they are taken seriously, and to develop social skills of arguing and reasoning, the more they are likely to be able to question assumptions about 'femininity' or 'masculinity', 'race' or 'culture'.

If secondary schools are to be enabled to change towards a more truly comprehensive approach we need to analyse and understand their structural basis as institutions in the light of greater awareness and knowledge of issues of inequality. It is particularly necessary to look at whole school structures, because the impact of changes effected by individual teachers or departments can be rendered less effective if contradicted by the messages pupils receive elsewhere in the school.

Strategies for change

Policy and structure
There are a number of problems to be tackled when it comes to taking on

issues of gender and race as part of whole school change. One is that race and gender have tended to be presented as specific policies to deal with overt problems that arise, such as harassment, violence and abuse — disruptions to the otherwise supposedly tolerant and peaceful life of the school. Regarded as such, race and gender issues tend to remain seen as separate from the real 'nitty gritties' of curriculum, timetabling and staffing, somewhat as marginal extras to be thought about after the basics have been dealt with. This is to some extent understandable in the light of the number of pressures on schools and the enormous difficulties of simply maintaining the status quo in the present climate. However, this level of operation is really one of responding to the symptoms of underlying problems. Outbursts of racist and sexist behaviour can be dealt with in the long term only by considering how racism and sexism can be examined through the whole curriculum and dealt with through the structures and practices of the school.

The permeation model
The apparently easy answer is that equality issues should permeate all planning and decision-making in the school and should form a central part of the thinking of all staff. This is not so easy in practice, partly because there are often genuinely conflicting interests to be met within limited resources. For example, the strong concern of one department to improve the performance of girls might lead them to decide on a policy of single sex groupings for a particular year group. However, the availability of staff or low numbers of pupils might make the formation of two groups, one for boys and one for girls, demanding in terms of resources. The final decisions on issues such as this are often far from clear cut, and are most often a combination of prioritizing and pragmatism. The decision as to what is in the best overall interest of everyone might be in conflict with the interests and needs of a particular group. This raises the question of the structures and processes for consultation and how these are managed in the school.

There is also the question of what constitutes knowledge and understanding of gender and race issues, not to mention varying levels of agreement with official policy among individuals. In large schools many decisions have to be delegated to a range of people. Not all of these will necessarily be in the vanguard of those staff who have undergone inservice training in equal opportunities, who have had the inclination or opportunity to educate themselves in this area, or who are committed out of personal or professional interest or experience. Some staff in positions of responsibility for decision-making may, although going along with official policy publicly, be personally opposed to positive steps to promote race and sex equality. Thus, all too easily, the permeation model can be a recipe for ignoring or glossing over urgent questions of gender and race, leaving individual teachers to do 'the best they can' within an unsatisfactory framework.

Effective models

Some of the more effective examples of whole school change have been where equality issues have been taken up as part of the formal structure of the school. This has involved establishing committees representing each department and pastoral team, who have been responsible to a senior member of staff with a specific brief for equal opportunities, with consultation and active involvement of other staff through the departments and year teams. An effective structural basis such as this avoids the danger of equal opportunities becoming the concern of a peripheral committed group of staff only, with limited influence and no official mechanisms for influencing school policy. However, for a formal structural model to effect genuine change requires real concern and support for equal opportunities from those in middle and senior management positions. In many schools this process has been preceded by years of painfully hard work, consciousness-raising and persuasion at grass roots level by groups of committed teachers.

Demystifying the curriculum

A major goal for such institutional change would be to affect radically the achievement patterns of black pupils, girls and working-class pupils. This involves a great deal of rethinking of how the curriculum is presented. It is not enough to say that we provide an accessible curriculum for all if some students are lacking in confidence and motivation, unable to organize their work or to persevere on account of a poor self-image. They will remain confused, dissatisfied and 'turned off' and consequently their learning will be blocked. As Sterling (1986) has argued, building pupils' self-confidence means demystifying the learning process through effective pupil-teacher communication and starting from where the pupil is, gradually building up confidence and skills. Looking at the different areas of achievement, including practical, personal and social skills and motivation has proved a useful approach in many schools (Hargreaves,1984).

Classroom organization

An equally important aspect of the curriculum is the way in which learning in the classroom is organized, and here pupil-centred and collaborative learning are central issues. The process and methods of assessment, including pupil assessment, are also highly relevant. Many teachers have found that girls work and perform better in a collaborative setting than in a situation of public competition. However, many boys experience difficulty in learning to work co-operatively and collaboratively, as Askew (1986) has documented. Research has also shown that girls are disadvantaged in examinations by multiple choice questions, and perform better at extended writing (Murphy, 1982). Similarly, many pupils whose first language is not English are disadvantaged in tests and assessment because of the language medium involved in testing other skills and competences. The question of cultural bias in tests and examinations is highly significant here.

In-service training and education
The development of effective teaching strategies, together with an awareness of the strong but subtle messages of the 'hidden curriculum', requires time and opportunity for teachers to reassess their aims, objectives and practice. One model which has proved effective in relation to equal opportunities is to combine theoretical understanding, through reading and discussion of academic research, with practical research by teachers in their own schools. Through structured school-based research projects such as interviews with pupils or staff, classroom observation, photography of the school environment, teacher researchers have seen and understood for themselves how gender, race and class operate — through the peer group, pupil interaction and groupings, resistance, and a whole range of pupil knowledge and experience of which teachers are often unaware (Adams and Arnot, 1986). Such understanding is empowering for teachers who are interested in changing school practices. It is also important that this knowledge is shared and disseminated widely among staff in the school and that it leads to forward planning for whole school change based on teachers' findings.

Parents and community links
Schools in which the need for positive steps to enhance the confidence and self-esteem of all pupils has become a priority have involved parents and others in the community. This has included not only consultation in policy making but actively enlisting parents' contributions to whole school events such as careers conventions and to curricular work as role models and living examples of the range of skills and expertise that exist in the local community. Securing parental support has been crucial to the success of projects set up to meet the needs of particular groups of pupils. For example one member of Shejuti, an East London Asian Girls' Youth Project, said: 'Parental learning is one of the side effects of Shejuti which goes on to affect the entire community' (Shejuti, 1986).

The current climate

Positive and lasting change to promote sex and race equality takes a great deal of hard work and time to get established. The current political climate and its expression through the media certainly does nothing to help this struggle to get equality issues accepted as part of the mainstream concerns of education. A common and somewhat predictable response to equal opportunities work over the last couple of years in the popular press has been to dismiss or ridicule it as the work of the 'lunatic fringe' which drains away resources from the 'real concerns' of parents and right-minded people *(The Times Educational Supplement,* 7 November 1986). It is a simplistic but most effective rallying cry. For if the public has access to little or no information about measures which have been taken in schools to enhance the quality of education and levels of achievement for all, how can they be expected to resist vote-catching slogans about returning to the supposed high standards of the past? It has been quite breathtaking how even the 'quality' press has avidly sought from documents and publications on equal opportunities examples which can be quoted out of context and distorted in order to undermine such work *(The Times Educational Supplement,* 29 July 1986).

A stage further from the 'return to basics' cry is the claim that those who are opposed to sexism and racism are engaged in social engineering towards 'the fraudulent ideal — essentially totalitarian — of equality and social justice' *(Daily Telegraph,* 1 July 1985). The implication is, of course, that those who are indifferent to or opposed to race and sex equality in education are politically neutral, unmotivated and essentially just.

Implications for the future

The realization of a genuinely comprehensive system of education requires urgent and thorough-going change in the interests of the majority of children. These changes are as necessary for rural white schools as for inner-city multi-racial schools, for single sex girls' and boys' schools as for mixed ones. They are long overdue. They challenge many assumptions and strongly held beliefs among those of us who have succeeded through the system. It is important to acknowledge that such change is already taking place in some schools and among many teachers. But our greatest hope for change is the pupils themselves. There is an urgent need for strategies to involve them in moving forward educational practice that will facilitate equal opportunities for all.

Issues of sex, race and class should form part of the overt curriculum, involving pupils as part of their education for a changing society. Much of what has been argued here has concentrated on the more structural aspects of policy and planning for the school and outcomes in terms of achievement. But just as important is the everyday experience of pupils as part of the school community, and the pastoral aspects of schooling which affect motivation and self esteem. If pupils are educated for understanding of the complexities of race, gender and class issues, not as unpleasant 'isms' to be punished when manifested during school hours (or more likely kept below the surface), but as major social issues in which they have a personal stake, then the principles of equality are more likely to become part and parcel of the comprehensives of the future. Students know about these issues already, as teachers who listen well know, but the school can either foster and cultivate this knowledge as an essential part of the education of the whole person, or negate it.

Where this understanding has been developed consciously by the school, so that pupils themselves take ownership of the issues and themselves take violation of individual or group rights seriously, written policy does become reality. I would suggest that in our debates and deliberations over the future of secondary schooling, the involvement of pupils through open discussion both within and beyond the formal curriculum should be given the highest priority. The majority of them have little to lose and everything to gain.

Acknowledgement
I should like to thank Richard Noss for his help in the preparation of this chapter.

References
Adams, C. and Arnot, M. (1986), *Investigating Gender in Secondary Schools.* London: Inner London Education Authority.

Arnot, M. (1983), 'A cloud over coeducation: an analysis of the forms of transmission of class and gender relations', in S. Walker and L. Barton (eds.), *Gender, Class and Education.* Lewes: Falmer Press.

Askew, S. (1986) 'Challenging images of masculinity in boys' schools', in C. Adams (ed.), *Secondary Issues.* London: Inner London Education Authority.

Assessment of Performance Unit (1986), *Girls and Physics.* APU

Centre for Contemporary Cultural Studies (1981), *Unpopular Education.* London: Hutchinson.

Delamont, S. (1980), *Sex Roles and the School*. London: Methuen.

Eccleston, J. (1985), 'The influence of school processes on the educational opportunities of children of West Indian origin', *Multicultural Teaching,* Vol. 4 No. 1.

Hargreaves, D. (1984), *Improving Secondary Schools,* London: Inner London Education Authority.

Isaacson, Z. (1986), 'Freedom and girls' education: a philosophical discussion with particular reference to mathematics', in L. Burton (ed.), *Girls into Maths Can Go.* Eastbourne: Holt, Rinehart and Winston.

McRobbie, A. (1978), 'Working class girls and the culture of femininity', in Centre for Contemporary Cultural Studies (eds.), *Women Take Issue.* London: Hutchinson.

Murphy, R. (1982), 'Sex differences in objective test performance', *British Journal of Educational Psychology,* Vol. 52.

Newsom, J. (1963), *Half Our Future.* London: HMSO.

Pratt, J., Bloomfield, J. and Seale, C. (1984), *Option Choice.* Windsor: NFER/Nelson.

Sharpe, S. (1976), *Just Like a Girl.* Harmondsworth: Pelican.

Shejuti young women (1986), 'Shejuti' in C. Adams (ed.), *Secondary Issues.* London: Inner London Education Authority.

Spender, D. and Elizabeth, S. (eds.) (1980), *Learning to Lose.* London: Women's Press.

Stanworth, M. (1983), *Gender and Schooling.* London: Hutchinson.

Sterling, R. (1986), 'Demystifying learning for equal opportunities', in C. Adams (ed.), *Secondary Issues.* London: Inner London Education Authority.

Willis, P. (1978), *Learning to Labour.* Aldershot: Gower.

Wright, C. (1985), 'Who succeeds at school — and who decides?' *Multicultural Teaching,* Vol 4, No. 1.

_____ (1987), 'The relationships between teachers and Afro-Caribbean pupils: observing multi-racial classrooms', in G. Weiner and M. Arnot (eds.), *Gender under Scrutiny: new inquiries in education:* London: Hutchinson.

Note

The views in this paper are those of the author, and in no way represent the views of the Inner London Education Authority.

Towards a Comprehensive Model for 16-19 Education

Margaret Maden

What I want to argue in this chapter* is that some of the policies for the education of sixteen-to-nineteen year olds now being considered do not take sufficient account of the young people themselves. In particular, these policies often seem to be predicated on versions and visions of economic reconstruction; they fail to consider sufficiently the desirability of matching the needs and characteristics of sixteen-to nineteen students to proposed organizational forms, or, indeed, to the detailed business of the 'what' and 'how' of effective learning for this age group. This is not, of course, an 'either/or': more, I think, a matter of an imbalance in current thinking.

In the first part of the chapter I shall say something about who these young people are, and from my own experience of working with them over the past four years put forward some ideas about their educational needs and entitlements. I shall then suggest one or two things about appropriate and inappropriate organizational forms and structures.

★　　★　　★

So who are they, these young people?

First, they are not children: nor are they fully adult. As young adults they are in a transitional state. In Germany at the moment there is much discussion about the need for *medial institutions* which recognize this fact. The sixteen-to-nineteen year olds are moving, one hopes progressing, from school with its more prescribed and authoritarian norms, to more specialist education or training, or to employment — each of which, after the age of eighteen, denotes a clearer adult status in law. Young people at this stage are in a

*A revised version of a speech delivered to the North of England Education Conference in January 1987.

state of relative dependence, economically, domestically, socially and educationally. Some cling to the apparent advantages of dependence; some fight it aggressively, often obnoxiously; many do both.

For parents and educators the turbulence of relations often seems a 'no win' situation. However, a recognition that this is a time when the young person needs and wants to explore his or her own identity provides an important framework within which growth and learning can flourish. Personal relationships within the peer group and with adults, sexual identity, sorting out social, moral and political values: these are matters of intense concern to all students.

At the Islington Sixth-Form Centre we have observed this commonality of concerns and preoccupations amongst our students — irrespective of previous school or level of academic achievement. And the educational strategies which are deployed to deal with these matters are crucial.

I am personally against the individualist approach often organized through the provision of one-to-one counselling. This is needed, but not as an exclusive or primary strategy. Rather it is the *institutional requirements and expectations* which set the scene for the genuine social and personal development of the young adult.

Rather than simply 'tacking on' counselling and advisory systems which are frequently rooted in the notion that young people have some awkward 'personal problems', my contention is that everything the institution or organization does should express a coherent set of assumptions and philosophies concerning the student's young adult status. These need to be rooted in a proper understanding of late adolescence as well as in a range of objectives which relate to a variety of desirable kinds of learning. The young person's need to acquire career qualifications which have genuine currency out there in the economic world is important. However, it is both foolish and utterly wrong-headed to deny the importance of a broader-based education which, in any case, *strengthens* the student's career prospects and pays due regard to the young person's right to be fulfilled as a social being and as a citizen. Man — or woman — does not live by bread alone; neither does a democracy flourish when *education* is for the few, narrow skill-based *training* for the many.

★   ★   ★

Here are a few and not particularly complicated examples of what I mean from my experience at the Islington Sixth-Form Centre. Before choosing a 'main course', be it B/TEC, CPVE, 'Access' or A level, we first of all set out 'ground rules' which are designed to convey to the student the distinctive nature of the institution as a place for sixteen-to-nineteen year olds.

First, we signal *our professional role* and the potential *student's personal responsibility* through a two-week course guidance workshop. The student negotiates a series of course 'tasters' which can involve him or her in two to five days of investigations into a variety of possible courses. The staff responsible for each 'taster' talk to the student concerned and provide a brief written comment on his or her suitability for the course. Finally, however, and following a summative discussion, it is the *student's* responsibility to choose a course.

The terms on which the student then enrols are clearly stated and are not especially remarkable, except that they require detailed monitoring and follow-up if they are to have more than symbolic meaning. The terms of this contract are (1) a 90 per cent attendance at all classes and tutorials; (2) full punctuality for all classes, tutorials, etc.; (3) regular completion of all work assignments; (4) a proper respect for other members of the Centre and for the Centre's fabric, equipment, etc.

The student is thus provided with a few basic prescriptions which are essentially connected with the *purpose* of being there. If he or she does not wish to be in the Centre's buildings when a free, non-timetabled, morning occurs, then that is his or her decision — but the work still has to be done. It is also made clear that it is the student's responsibility to signal any difficulties s/he may experience in the study programme by talking directly to the teacher concerned or to the personal tutor. Of course it is not quite as simple as this, mainly because most sixteen-year-olds are not used to assuming responsibility for their own learning; nor have they acquired the skills needed to complain or explain effectively. The students also negotiate their *short course* programme which is meant to relate to both their personal interests and development and to extension or support work needed for improved performance in their main course.

To our surprise the weekly *tutorial meeting* has proved to be both popular and strongly educational. This contrasts markedly with my earlier eleven-to-eighteen comprehensive school experience when tutor group time was something of a 'black hole' we all rather dreaded.

Tutor group meetings occur simultaneously on a Friday morning. It is a bit like a mass 'town crier' event — all the business of the Centre as an educational community is dealt with. A common agenda is provided by the Deputy Director (Student Services); staff and students contribute to it. Reports from the Student Council, from the governors, from staff-student working parties or from students who have just emerged from a period of work experience or a residential visit are included. Complaints from the Head of Kitchen or Schoolkeeper may arise. Ideas culled from recent visiting speakers, ranging from the local police commander through to such luminaries as Sir Keith Joseph, Lady Antonia Fraser or Ken Livingstone, are further debated and dissected. All of these are presented as 'house business' and there will frequently be a larger, more distant political or moral issue presented for discussion. But all provide the tutor and students with grist for democratic debate.

In these ways it is the *students who increasingly shape the institution;* the teachers are guides and mentors, neither authoritarian nor obtrusive beyond the stated terms of the 'contract'. This is an effective form of social and political education: important at any stage, but especially with sixteen-to-nineteen year olds, and essentially rooted in *the nature of the institution.*

★   ★   ★

Two further and related matters should be added at this point, concerning the institution's response to the sixteen-to-nineteen year old student. (I have outlined the role of the tutor and of the teaching staff in the Sixth-Form Centre's course guidance process.)

The teacher, of course, spends most of his or her time *teaching,* whether this takes place in BTEC technician studies, CPVE business administration or A-level history. The need for concentrated attention to the learning requirements of students who have recently emerged from school cannot be over-estimated. The weaning from a more dependent style of learning to a more autonomous, self-directed style is not at all simple. As students learn how to learn, they come to understand more fully the distinction between what is and what is not worth knowing — and this applies to *all* students. Because most courses are of one or two years' duration and because I am assuming, for a variety of reasons, a change of institution at sixteen, a high priority is clearly that of specialist and focused teaching — not so much specialist in the sense of subject expertise (though this matters), but more in the sense of specialist teaching in relation to sixteen-to-nineteen year olds. Understanding and appreciating the recent education experience of sixteen or seventeen year olds as well as their current preoccupations and characteristics forms the basis of effective teaching in this phase. In the Inner London Education Authority we hope to make some joint appointments of teaching staff between our tertiary colleges and their partner schools to strengthen this key link and need for some continuity.

A similar expertise needs to exist in relation to the economic, personal and social aspirations of the student. Each of these, the past, present and likely future of students and the medial nature of the present task, influences and shapes the style of teaching, as well as the selection of syllabuses and options. Thus, where the student has come from, what his or her needs and concerns are between the age of sixteen, eighteen or nineteen, and where s/he is heading, represent a critical set of pedagogic imperatives sufficient to keep even the most talented teacher fully occupied — and stretched.

★   ★   ★

A final characteristic of this age group is the existence of parents. In law at least, the parent still has a role up to the eighteenth birthday of the child. It is curious that the present Government is so concerned to promote and expand the rights of parents in relation to the statutory period of education in schools, but not, it appears, to the increasing number of institutions operating under FE regulations where more and more students under the age of eighteen are to be found. This probably relates to the fact that the Government (and probably the Labour Party also) sees the major stakeholder in FE as employers, or 'Industry'; parents figure only as potential 'blockers' of tertiary reorganization schemes.

Just as parents who pay for their children to attend independent schools as sixth formers expect to be involved in (or at least informed about) the progress of their offspring, so should the parents of sixteen-to-eighteen year old students in FE or tertiary colleges. The rights of parents to receive full and standardized information about schools, including examination results, rules, arrangements for consultation, should surely be extended to FE and tertiary colleges; in these cases for potential students and employers as well as for parents. Similarly, the expectation that parents sign before a young person enters an apprenticeship should apply to a young person on a YTS programme.

The *form* of the institutional or organizational relationship with parents needs to be thought about in the same way as does the relationship with the student. Parents need educating and inducting often as much as, or more than, the young person. The agonies experienced by many parents of sixteen or seventeen-year olds are worth a study on its own. It is obviously desirable that parents *are* kept informed about their child's progress and the involvement of the student in such informing and parental consultations is to me a necessary component in such transactions.

To mark the changing relationship between parent and young adult, it is **important that a student educational grant or allowance is provided as a basic** right. This is needed to express a student's more adult and autonomous status; it is also a matter of dire practical necessity for many students, expecially those who have traditionally not chosen, or been able to choose, further education.

★　　★　　★

Some thoughts, now, about institutional forms and organizational principles and the provision of a truly comprehensive experience. I am unequivocally in favour of a break at sixteen, and I am equally strong in my support of an extension of comprehensive education beyond sixteen. These two principles lead me to support a tertiary system based on a variety of tertiary colleges. My main reasons for favouring a change of institution at sixteen are based on both my own experience and on national evidence. Briefly, both participation rates and performance levels improve, not least because the young person positively responds to the opportunities offered in the more mature learning environment of an institution designed to serve his or her needs. Of course, *any* kind of break at sixteen is not the answer, but rather a carefully designed provision which contains a good deal of expertise relating to the requirements of young adults.

Unfortunately the recent DES draft circular, 'Providing the quality: the pattern of organization to age 19', fails to provide the quality promised in its title. When the Secretary of State says 'preserve the best, improve the rest', I interpret this in my own way. Preserving the best does not mean to me preserving sixth forms 'of proven worth'; rather it means developing and reinterpreting the best features of the sixth form for *all* young people. It also means dispensing with the worst and most debilitating aspects of the sixth form as a cultural ideology.

We need to remind ourselves that the sixth form began as a radical innovation linked to fundamental changes in politics and society in the nineteenth century. Its subsequent history is that of an evolving category which has always built the new on what already existed in order to maintain the significance of its forms and activities; a significance which has always related to status enhancement rather than skill enhancement.

The *main* purpose of an educational system in a democratic society is, I believe, to provide a means of incorporating citizens into a public activity concerned with the furtherance of the common interest. Educational systems also perform other necessary functions, such as conveying essential knowledge or regulating the passage of students from schooling to employment, but where there is an overriding concern for democratic ideals then *the goal of incorporation takes precedence.*

What needs to be rejected in the still-powerful sixth-form ideology is its peculiar notion of incorporating an elite rather than *all* young people. In practical terms this means organizing matters so that the shared needs and concerns of young people are given precedence, whether the student is in part-time or full-time attendance, whether he or she is pursuing a course validated by GCE, B/TEC or by the MSC, and whether he or she is black or white, male or female, comes from a special school, comprehensive school or independent school.

Thus, the concept of the sixth form as a school within a school, as a 'moral aristocracy', has to go. Reid and Filby comment in their book, *The Sixth: an essay in education and democracy,*

> there is a need to ensure that education systems are truly educational in that they aim to engender capacities rather than teach competences, and that they encourage in all people feelings of full membership in the commonwealth rather than show on what grounds membership is to be confined or limited (Reid and Filby, 1982, p.6).

It is unfortunate that heads of secondary schools are currently preoccupied with more immediately pressing problems than the issues I raise here. Distilling and analyzing the sixth-form tradition, sorting out the good from the bad, should be their contribution to the evolution of a stronger and more democratic form of sixteen-to-nineteen education. Neither strident unthinking reaction against the loss of sixth forms nor a fatalistic acquiescence in what is frequently recognized as the inevitable loss of sixth forms is a good enough response.

For a variety of reasons — both intended and unitended — the first wave of tertiary colleges has successfully combined the virtues of accessibility and adaptability with the desirable aspects of the sixth form's coherence and high status — with more and more public support. Because these colleges were initially established with the needs of sixteen-to-nineteen year olds as their primary concern, they represent an increasingly successful example of what I have earlier described as a *medial institution* characterized by maturity, realism and democracy. Now, however, that many tertiary schemes are being proposed in areas where the sixteen-to-nineteen year olds will be either a minority or near-minority group in the constituent colleges, I feel that this hard-won evolution is in danger of being destroyed.

Where the educational purposes of an institution are very diverse, I think it is still an open question whether the interests of sixteen-to-nineteen year olds will be properly served, especially where there is a real danger of 'institutional overload', trying to do too much and diffusing to an intolerable degree the tasks of the institution.

In the case of young people in the inner city, it also seems to be especially true that their educational institutions need to be *educational communities* — perhaps because other communities no longer exist, except in soap operas such as *East Enders*. Hence notions of institutional membership and coherence are important — and for *all* sixteen-to-nineteen year olds there needs to exist an ethos or 'hidden curriculum' which systematically conveys the values and precepts crucial to the effective learning and maturing of young adults.

*   *   *

The growth of educational and training demands amongst the adult poplulation obviously deserve as much consideration and resource as do the needs of the sixteen-to-nineteen group. This is why I referred earlier to the need for a *tertiary system* based on a variety of tertiary colleges.

Comprehensive principles can, and in my view must, include a recognition of differences, but not the differences between academic or general education and 'vocational or skills training. There is, I believe, the real danger in some of our present arrangements that we shall increasingly produce a more divided system comprising 'academic sheep' and 'vocational goats'. The exclusion of GCSE, A and A/S level courses from the NCVQ remit will serve to strengthen this.

A broad-based education which includes the development of capacities needed to participate fully in a stronger democracy is needed for all young people whether they follow a YTS or an A-level programme. This would not exclude more specific education and training which, in any case, contributes to the more adult status of sixteen-to-nineteen year olds.

What better way to conclude than by citing a couple of appropriate, if now slightly arcane, quotations from Tawney. He wrote in his essay on *Equality* that it was important:

> to set the realities of child life in the centre of the stage, as the criterion by which all educational arrangements are to be tested; to adapt educational organization, not to social conventions or economic convenience, but to the requirements of the children (Tawney, 1931, p.142).

He further observed that:

> the boys and girls of well-to-do parents . . . continue their education as a matter of course, not because they are exceptional, but because they are normal and the question of the 'profit' they succeed in deriving from it is left, quite rightly, to be answered later. Working-class children have the same needs to be met and the same powers to be developed (ibid., p.143).

References

Reid, W. and Filby, J. (1982). *The Sixth: an essay in education and democracy.* Lewes: The Falmer Press.

Tawney, R. H. (1931), *Equality.* London: Unwin Books.

The Way Forward

Clyde Chitty

> Reflecting upon the magnitude of the general evil, I should be oppressed with a dishonourable melancholy, had I not a deep impression of certain inherent and indestructible qualities of the human mind.

William Wordsworth: *Lyrical Ballads, 1798-1805*, Preface.

> . . . One would have said beyond a doubt
> That was the very end of the bout,
> But that the creature would not die.

Edwin Muir: 'The Combat'.

To return to the questions posed in the first chapter: why is so much energy being devoted to the cause of undermining public confidence in our comprehensive system of secondary education; and why is the Government so determined to intensify the process of differentiation *within* and *between* schools?

After all, judged by the narrow criterion of examination success alone, comprehensive schools would appear to have done remarkably well. We learn, for example, from *Better Schools* (DES, 1985a, p.3) that in 1983 one in five students gained at least one GCE A-level pass, compared with one in seven during the 1960s, and that over a quarter of pupils obtained five O-level 'pass' equivalents against a fifth twenty or so years ago. At the same time, nearly half the school population now receives full-time education until at least the age of seventeen, compared with one in eight in 1947 (ibid., p.2). And more recent statistics show that the percentage of teenagers leaving school with no graded results at O level or CSE was 11.7 per cent in 1984/85, compared with 13.5 per cent in 1980/81 and 44 per cent in 1970/71 (DES, 1986).

Simon has argued (1984, p.20) that 'the very success of comprehensive secondary schooling — as opposed to the myth of its "failure" — has contributed to accelerating the clear and energetic thrust of both the present Government and DES officials to greatly enhanced central control'. One of the main objectives of Civil Servants and Government officials has clearly been the enhancement of differentiated learning experiences *within* individual comprehensive schools. Even the HMI document *The Curriculum from 5 to 16,* published in 1985, talks in terms of the ideal curriculum having four main characteristics: breadth, balance, relevance, and differentiation (DES, 1985b, pp.42-7). Separate categories of education from at least the age of fourteen will, of course, restrict the educational opportunities available in our schools. In Simon's view, 'the argument for centralizing powers is based on the need for explicit social engineering to cope with the dangers arising from over-education in a contracting labour market'. And he makes use of research carried out by Ranson (1984, pp.221-44) into the thinking of senior DES officials to back up his thesis. In Ranson's paper, more than one DES official is shown to be quite open about the need to achieve fully centralized power and control for the sake of social harmony:

> There has to be selection because we are beginning to create aspirations which increasingly society cannot match. In some ways, this points to the success of education in contrast to the public mythology which has been created. When young people drop off the education production line and cannot find work at all, or work which meets their abilities or expectations, then we are only creating frustrations with perhaps disturbing social consequences. We have to select: to ration the educational opportunities to meet the job opportunities so that society can cope with the output of education.

and:

> We are in a period of considerable social change. There may be social unrest, but we can cope with the Toxteths. But if we have a highly educated and idle population, we may possibly anticipate more serious social conflict. Poeple must be educated once more to know their place.

The supporters of the New Right also want children to be educated once more to 'know their place' in the social hierarchy, but they believe this can be achieved through the free and unfettered operation of market forces.

To answer the critics of the Right and the 'social manipulators' of the DES, we need both to highlight and build upon the successes of comprehensive education *and* to find ways of utilizing and exploiting current government strategies, however retrograde, for democratic and progressive ends.

★   ★   ★

Exciting developments are taking place, for example, in the growing number of genuine community colleges, not just along lines advocated by Henry Morris in Cambridgeshire (whose colleges are now seen as being at the 'traditional' end of the community education spectrum) but also in radical and pioneering directions inspired, particularly, by the needs of inner-city and priority areas. Writing about the 'golden age' of Sutton Centre in Nottinghamshire from 1973 to 1977, Fletcher says: 'comprehensive education developed because of an ethos of community education. Content was more important than form. How people got on with each other was rated more highly than how they were separated into tasks and statuses. In sum, rather than a replica of a secondary modern or grammar school, or a little of both, there was a different kind of school'. (Fletcher, 1981, p.156) More recently, Community Vice-Principal Paddy Hall has described the work of Moat Community College situated in the Highfields area of Leicester where of the 1,100 or so pupils, 13 per cent are Afro-Caribbean, 11 per cent Europeans and 75 per cent of Asian descent. He shows how, in terms of both curriculum and community activities, the College is developing multicultural and, above all, anti-racist approaches:

> Multiculturalism on its own runs the risk of being purely decorative, unless accompanied by much stronger anti-racist policies and activities . . . Racism is prejudice with power. It is a symptom of fear and weakness, not of strength. Education has not led society in this country for a long time. It has reflected it, good and ill. Perhaps, optimistically, community education is in a position to give away a little of the power, ease by contact a little of the fear, and begin, with local people as allies, to give prejudice a good kicking! (Hall, 1986, p.38)

It is interesting to note that when Sir Keith Joseph visited the College in the wake of the 1981 disturbances, one of his chief concerns was that the teachers were not doing enough to encourage a sense of patriotism!

We have, of course, to accept the criticism that, in general, our comprehensive schools have not done enough to enrich the learning process for *all* pupils. Bernard Barker has argued the case for a content-led curriculum but he deplores the continuing domination of the academic grammar-school model. As was noted in the first chapter, the HMI report of 1979 concluded that the switch to comprehensive education and the raising of the school leaving age had not resulted in any fundamental rethinking of the secondary curriculum and consequently many students, both the very able and the less able, were following courses of study which were too narrow. Bob Moon, Head of Peers School in Oxford, has argued that the option system operating in years four and five of most comprehensives has always been part of the 'deference' curriculum evolved in the 1960s to ensure that the grammar-school curriculum was perpetuated within the comprehensive school (Moon, 1984, pp.35-8). And using data collected in a community in Wales in the mid-1970s, the authors of *The Comprehensive Experiment* conclude that the academic emphasis, pressure and ethos of the comprehensive schools studied generated a counter-reaction from amongst their lower-ability pupils.

> As schools, the comprehensives had not managed to reach the accommodations with pupils reached in the secondary moderns, and consequently as grammar schools for all, they were unable to hold or socially control those pupils for whom the grammar school and its academic traditions were a notable irrelevance (Reynolds, Sullivan and Murgatroyd, 1987, pp.108-9).

In putting forward an alternative perspective and, at the same time, taking account of recent developments in curriculum and pedagogy, we are, in fact, acknowledging that the academic curriculum model was highly unsuitable for large numbers of pupils in the first generation of comprehensives. But that is not an argument for taking on board the thinking behind the New Vocationalism which simply replaces one narrow focus of learning (academic) with another (practical and vocational). We need to see curriculum development in terms of a synthesis between the academic, the vocational, the technical and the practical. It was *Curriculum 11-16,* published in 1977 and subsequently described as 'Red Book 1', which first gave an opportunity for Her Majesty's Inspectorate to outline the case for 'a common curriculum in secondary education to sixteen' and identify eight areas of experience (subsequently increased to nine) as the best means of achieving this. The HMI model curriculum of 1977 would comprise: the aesthetic and creative; the ethical; the linguistic; the mathematical; the physical; the scientific; the social and political; and the spiritual (DES, 1977, p.6). The third of the HMI Red Books, published in 1983, explored this idea further and now talked in terms of an 'entitlement curriculum':

> It seemed essential that *all* pupils should be guaranteed a curriculum of a distinctive breadth and depth to which they should be *entitled,* irrespective of the type of school they attended or their level of ability or their social circumstances and that failure to provide such a curriculum is unacceptable . . . The conviction has grown that all pupils are entitled to a broad compulsory common curriculum to the age of sixteen which introduces them to a range of experiences, makes them aware of the kinds of society in which they are going to live and gives them the skills necessary to live in it. Any curriculum which fails to provide this balance and is overweighted in any particular direction, whether vocational, technical or

academic, is to be seriously questioned. Any measures which restrict the access of all pupils to a wide-ranging curriculum or which focus too narrowly on specific skills are in direct conflict with the entitlement curriculum envisaged here (DES, 1983, pp.25, 26).

Far from setting out, then, to reverse the comprehensive revolution, we should seek to continue and develop it as the means of providing all pupils with a curriculum which is liberating and worthwhile. As Ranson, Taylor and Brighouse have pointed out (1986, p.2), this involves arguing for greater recognition of different kinds of achievement, for a broadening and modular organizing of the curriculum, for non-didactic forms of teaching and for flexible modes of assessment which credit achievement and enable progression. 'Individually many of the elements of reform are not new, but taken together they constitute an agenda of action and an emergent revolution in the experience of learning.' While recent Government initiatives reflect a negative philosophy encouraging selection and a narrow, utilitarian experience, they have to be 'transformed' at school or college level to constitute genuine educational advance.

★   ★   ★

The Technical and Vocational Education Initiative has clearly been a divisive influence in many schools, but it has also meant the allocation of funds to a number of worthwhile and innovative projects. At Ysgol Emrys ap Iwan in Abergele, for example, TVEI, when it arrived in 1983, proved to be a facilitator. The school was able to set up electronics laboratories and a computer suite with expensive equipment as well as providing office furnishing for a number of vocational courses. TVEI also facilitated the retention and extension of a modular curriculum which, in the words of an external evaluation undertaken by Susan Pyart, 'has made fundamental changes' to the whole life and ethos of the school' (Ysgol Emrys ap Iwan, 1986).

Real advance can also be made *within* the new GCSE framework. As I have argued elsewhere (Mortimore, Mortimore and Chitty, 1986), there are clearly ways in which the new structure of examining, with all its drawbacks, can still incorporate flexible and progressive features. The courses taken by the pupils can be broken down into units, thereby utilizing a modular approach; assessments can be provided at appropriate points; and achievements can be recorded and stored in the profiles of the pupils, which will then constitute a continuous record of their progress through the later years of secondary school. The GCSE might well be an initiative which does not have the desired effect of undermining teacher autonomy. There is evidence that the DES is already concerned that there is more continuous assessment in the new GCSE system than was originally intended. And Kenneth Baker has found it necessary to reassure businessmen that this will not, in fact, lead to a lowering of standards. Speaking in May 1987 in Guildford, Surrey, at the first of a series of conferences to promote confidence in the exam, he made clear his own lack of confidence in teachers' professional standards: 'to guard against bias, conscious or unconscious, and to protect standards, the new system will include a very thorough audit system' (quoted in the *Guardian,* 6 May 1987).

An example of how progress is possible *within* the current framework is provided by the county of Oxfordshire. It was in 1986 that the Oxfordshire Examinations Syndicate was set up as an imaginative attempt to give teachers and schools genuine control over the GCSE. It started as the brainchild of a group of heads, teachers and local authority advisers. According to Mike Jones, Principal of Wantage School and chairperson of the project's executive group: 'Our first response to the GCSE was that it would be a step backwards, putting a brake on developments in our schools . . . Then we realized we could seize the chance in the two years before something was imposed on us and set in concrete.' The main purpose of the syndicate is to set up a bank of short courses or credits that can be mixed and matched for different GCSE certificates, either building to traditional subject certificates or to newer interdisciplinary ones in science, humanities or the creative arts. The syndicate is working in close association with the Southern Examining Group (SEG), which will act as guardian of the national criteria, helping to vet credits and decide which fit together for different certificates. Although Oxfordshire is not the first local authority to try to devise an accredited system for modular GCSE courses, developments in the county have been led to a unique extent by the schools and teachers themselves (Makins, 1987).

More flexible approaches to the recording of achievement could actually be in line with government policy. In 1984, the Government endorsed experiments already under way in some schools and local authorities to develop methods of giving school-leavers a fuller record of their school achievements than a single certificate of public exam passes or failures: it provided funds for ten further pilot schemes. The aim is that by the end of the decade, all school-leavers should receive an agreed summary of everything they have achieved in school. Several examination boards and local authorities are now working on large-scale schemes, such as the Oxford Certificate of Educational Achievement (OCEA), validated by the Oxford

Delegacy for Local Examinations. These could well be useful developments, provided they are not restricted to specific groups of supposedly low-achieving pupils.

★   ★   ★

On the question of the national curriculum, it has been argued (Lawton, 1987; Lawton and Chitty, 1987) that it may not be too late to rescue the concept from the hands of the politicians. But it will need to be a professional model based upon 'areas of experience' and drawing on the expertise of teachers and HMI, rather than a crude bureaucratic model concentrating on a limited number of 'core' subjects and drawn up by the Civil Servants of the DES. Above all, we need to free the proposal for a centrally-imposed curriculum from the accompanying notion of age-related bench-mark testing which would simply act as a straitjacket on the entire system.

It is not necessarily the case, as the present Government seems to think, that we have much to learn in curriculum matters from our European neighbours. Reporting on their comparative study of France and England as typical of centralized and decentralized systems respectively, Broadfoot and Osborn have argued (1987, pp.18-19) that although some pupils succeed in the French system, 'the price is all too often a dull, repetitive and harsh pedagogy focused narrowly on the objectives that must be achieved if the pupils are to avoid repeating the year'. While English teachers, particularly at the primary level, concentrate on the needs and interests of each individual child, the view of French teachers is that 'their job is essentially unproblematic involving a fairly narrow emphasis on imparting the prescribed skills and knowledge to all pupils as far as possible equally and then measuring their success by the number of children achieving the required learning outcomes'. Broadfoot and Osborn argue that before we embark on a national curriculum, it would be sensible to examine the assumptions on which such a policy is based and the overall implications for our education system:

> It makes good sense to have some nationally-agreed curriculum objectives so that there is greater equality of opportunity for all pupils. But this idea should not be mixed up with national standards, testing and teacher accountability. If it is, the result is likely to be an unwarranted emphasis on teaching to the test and a substantial increase in the number of pupils who early in their school careers come to regard themselves as failures (ibid.).

★   ★   ★

There are, then, both contradictions and possibilities within the policies and rhetoric of the Right which have to be exploited on a number of levels. This point has been developed by my colleague Michael Young in his chapter on vocationalization. We have to take account, he argues, of the new education language of student-centred learning and negotiated curricula. Current policies may well embrace projects which have the potential of empowering students who would not have thought they had demands to make on the system.

But, of course, it will also be necessary to fight for comprehensive education at a political level. Recent Government proposals serve to remind us that the fight against selection is never finally won: it has to be refought by each succeeding generation of democrats and egalitarians. As Michael Fielding writes in his chapter (p.51): 'If we do not defend comprehensive schools successfully, if we do not unmask the pseudo-comprehensive discourse of Tory education policy, the gains which have been painfully won over decades will be undermined or reversed.' Not that the new proposals mean simply a return to the divided system of the immediate post-war period, damaging though that would be in itself. The Radical Right is now exerting enormous influence on Government education policy, and in its repudiation of the post-war social democratic consensus, the philosophy of this powerful caucus, rooted as it is in the open affirmation of 'free market values', requires that the state system of comprehensive education should be effectively dismantled. Education junior minister Bob Dunn told right-wing supporters within the Conservative Party in May 1987 that Government proposals to allow schools to take as many pupils as they could physically cope with, in tandem with plans to give heads control of school budgets and the right to 'opt out' of council control, were all parts of a strategy that would eventually lead to 'the denationalization of education' *(The Times Educational Supplement,* 15 May 1987). And at a pre-election press conference, Margaret Thatcher argued that heads and governing bodies who 'opted out' of local education authority control should be free to establish their own admissions policies and would not necessarily be prevented from raising extra funds through parents — thereby giving rise to much media speculation that the new plans might include a fee-paying element (reported in the *Guardian,* 23 May 1987). Indeed, Kenneth Baker conceded during a BBC Radio Four *World at One* discussion broadcast on 10 June 1987 that there would be nothing to stop better-off parents raising additional resources for a particular school so that the headteacher would be able to purchase expensive books and items of equipment and pay the teachers higher salaries. It must be of significance that Stuart Sexton, at one time chief policy adviser to Sir Keith Joseph, argued in his recently-published document *Our Schools: A Radical Policy* that the law should be changed 'to allow state-maintained schools to make reasonable charges, not for the education itself offered at the school, but for the "extras"' (Sexton, 1987, p.24).

The 1987 Conservative Party Election Manifesto, *The Next Moves Forward*, announced four major reforms in education, only one of which — the proposal to establish 'a national core curriculum' — could be said to reflect the preoccupations and concerns of the last ten years. The remaining three involve: governing bodies and headteachers of all secondary schools and many primary schools being given control over their own budgets; City Technology Colleges being established as a pilot scheme; and state schools being allowed to opt out of LEA control. There seems every reason to suppose that these proposals will form an important part of the new Education Bill to be introduced into the House of Commons in November.

It is fair to point out that much confusion still surrounds at least one of these proposals. At a press conference held after his speech to the Council of Local Education Authorities' Conference in Lancaster on 17 July, Kenneth Baker stated that if a school decided to opt out of local authority control, this must be regarded as an irrevocable decision. 'Opting out is a once-and-for-all choice', he said (reported in the *Guardian*, 18 July 1987). But a few hours later this view was flatly contradicted in a special press release issued by the DES which itself reiterated an earlier statement by the Education Secretary that a decision to opt out *could* be reversed after a number of years. In the circumstances, it is hardly surprising that the new Labour shadow education spokesperson, Jack Straw, felt able to comment in the BBC Radio Four *Today* programme on the morning of 18 July that Mr Baker appeared to be 'drafting education policy on the backs of envelopes — and then losing the envelopes'.

There can be little doubt that the 1987 election, with its huge Conservative victory, will turn out to have been a watershed in the history of post-war education. Here at last is the real break with the trends and developments of the past ten years. Asked by a caller to a pre-election radio and television programme in the BBC series *Election Call*, broadcast on 10 June 1987, what she regretted she had not actually achieved during eight years of Conservative government, the Prime Minister replied: 'In some ways, I wish we had begun to tackle education earlier. We have been content to continue the policies of our predecessors. But now we have much worse left-wing Labour authorities than we have ever had before — so something simply has to be done' (reported in the *Guardian*, 11 June 1987).

A number of moderate Conservatives will be natural allies in any campaign to preserve the state system of secondary education. The Conservative Education Association was launched at the end of March 1987 to campaign for a return to moderate, 'one-nation', consensus Conservatism. One of its leading members, Philip Merridale, the Conservative leader on the Council of Local Education Authorities, confessed that 'his blood chills' on hearing the rapturous applause that Kenneth Baker invariably receives from the Tory faithful when launching blistering attacks on local government. And another founding father, Professor Paul Wilkinson of Aberdeen University, confessed that he felt real alarm at the current direction of Government policy. 'There are some very dangerous ideas about. This is our last chance to defeat them. We are crusaders for education.' (reported in *The Times Educational Supplement*, 3 April 1987).

At the same time, a number of teacher unions have declared their readiness to participate in a national campaign to defend state education against privatization. According to Doug McAvoy, Deputy General Secretary of the National Union of Teachers, 'our priority now is to protect the education service. The best way to do that is to create a partnership with the local education authorities and parents.' And David Hart, General Secretary of the National Association of Head Teachers, has said his association will 'campaign vigorously against allowing schools to opt out of the state system.' In his view: 'it is not the answer to the problems of inner-city schooling; it is irrelevant . . . The real issue is money. If we are to have a national curriculum, attainment tests and budgetary devolution, they have to be resourced properly. My members are desperately worried about the widening gap between state and independent schools.'

★　　★　　★

As long ago as 1943, the Board of Education issued a White Paper, *Educational Reconstruction,* incorporating the following unequivocal statement:

> There is nothing to be said in favour of a system which subjects children at the age of eleven to the strain of a competitive examination on which, not only their future schooling, but their future careers may depend.

This was a bold statement for 1943 (albeit in a document whose general conclusions were anything but progressive); but it now needs to be extended to embrace any form of selection procedure at eleven.

Yet the notion of dividing youngsters up into neat ability groupings and then providing for them accordingly dies hard. The authors of *The Comprehensive Experiment* assert, admittedly on the basis of very limited findings, that comprehensive schools generally make a mistake in trying to formulate a common curriculum for all pupils. While they reject the idea of selection for different types of school at eleven and do not argue that comprehensives should be rigidly banded with each band following its own curriculum, they nonetheless feel that there should be a larger degree of differentiation within the common school.

> We do not agree with crude left-wing visions of the comprehensive school as a universal, common experience for all . . . We also do not agree with the extreme forms of selectivity under one roof which characterize Conservative visions of the schools, with a radically different curriculum and ethos existing for the top and lower parts of the ability range . . . For us, neither crude left nor right-wing visions of the school are sensible. Left-wing visions would generate too much uniformity — right-wing visions too many social differences. For us, the comprehensive school is to be both universalistic *and* selectivistic, with a common universal experience that is partially selectively modified or 'topped up' according to the different needs of portions of the ability ranges and of individuals within them. Our desired comprehensives are neither one model nor the other — they incorporate elements of both (Reynolds, Sullivan and Murgatroyd, 1987, p.130).

The Reynolds, Sullivan and Murgatroyd formula may appear superficially attractive — with its appeal to the British flair for compromise — but the danger lies in its inherent vagueness. It is all too easy for the identification of pupil needs to become a justification for totally differentiated curriculum provison. It is all too easy for ability groupings to become harsh and inflexible with pupils performing according to teacher expectations. If we are to derive full benefit from the comprehensive principle, we need to reject the whole idea of selection either of pupils or of curriculum content in favour of a concept which is positive and unifying. There can be no justification for imprisoning pupils at the age of eleven — or indeed, at any age — in courses marked exclusively 'academic' or 'practical' or 'vocational', at least in the sense in which those terms are currently understood. In the view of George Walker, Headteacher of The Cavendish School in Hertfordshire, writing in 1984:

> Out of diversity and compromise (has) begun to emerge a recognizable ideal that (can) provide the rationale of comprehensive education: the common curriculum . . . At its very best, a carefully constructed common curriculum to which the whole staff is committed guarantees to pupils *of all abilities* a balanced and relevant learning experience without all the unnecessary clutter that has accumulated over years of *ad hoc* curriculum planning (Walker, 1984, p.23).

Pupils should be allowed to learn at different paces using different strategies, but they will all be moving broadly along the same curricular pathway. To return to the theme of the third HMI Red Book: all pupils are *entitled* to a curriculum that is relevant, worthwhile and liberating. It must be a curriculum that is not frightened to tackle with sensitivity and intelligence all the complex moral and social issues of our times — including the nuclear issue and all the themes of gender, race and class which Carol Adams writes about in her chapter. It must be a curriculum that retains strong positive common elements to the age of sixteen so that all pupils can study complex and difficult issues which are not easily comprehended at an early age.

★　　★　　★

Simon has articulated the function of a comprehensive education in the following terms:

> Schools have the function of deliberately promoting not only the skills of numeracy and literacy, but, through a progressively deepening grasp of knowledge and culture, the autonomy of the student able to function effectively within society, and to use his or her abilities to change that society according to developing aspirations. Such a formation cannot happen by chance; nor by relying on supposed inborn or innate tendencies and abilities. It requires recognition of the formative power of education, the consequent definition of objectives, and identification of the means by which these objectives may be realized (Simon, 1980, p.13).

According to this analysis, it has to be the task of education to prepare students for something beyond immediate demands and horizons fore-shortened in job terms. And there would appear to be fairly broad agreement on the need to reject a narrowly utilitarian view of education. Reports recently from the Manpower Services Commission, the National Economic Development Council, the Confederation of British Industry and the British Institute of Management have all agreed that what industry most needs is a workforce with a good, broad education which industry itself can then build on with the right training at every level.

The comprehensive system does not, by itself, guarantee a decent education for all pupils, but without it, no further advance is possible. It is a system which can embrace a number of institutional arrangements: the traditional eleven-to-eighteen all-through schools (now somewhat out of favour, especially in the large cities); a system of eleven-to sixteen schools and tertiary colleges (for which Margaret Maden has argued forcibly in her chapter); a system with eight-to-twelve or nine-to-thirteen middle schools or eleven-to-fourteen junior high schools; and so on. Whatever form it takes, it is the only system which can demonstrate a clear faith in human potential and prevent the writing-off of large numbers of pupils as second-class citizens. The great need now is not only to defend the achievements of the past twenty years but also to build upon them in ways which provide enhanced opportunities for all the nation's children.

References

Board of Education (1943), *Educational Reconstruction* (White Paper), London: HMSO.

Broadfoot, P. and Osborn, M. (1987), 'French lessons', *The Times Educational Supplement,* 3 July.

Conservative Party (1987), *The Next Moves Forward.* London: Conservative Central Office, May.

DES (1977), *Curriculum 11-16* (HMI Red Book One). London: HMSO.

_____ (1979), *Aspects of Secondary Education in England: A Survey by HM Inspectors of Schools.* London: HMSO.

_____ (1983), *Curriculum 11-16: Towards a Statement of Entitlement: Curricular Reappraisal in Action* (HMI Red Book Three). London: HMSO.

_____ (1985a) *Better Schools.* London: HMSO, Cmnd. 9469.

_____ (1985b) *The Curriculum from 5 to 16,* Curriculum Matters 2 (an HMI series). London: HMSO.

_____ (1986), *Education Statistics for the United Kingdom 1986.* London: HMSO.

Fletcher, C. (1981), 'A community school', in L. Barton, and S. Walker (eds.), *Schools, Teachers and Teaching.* Lewes: Falmer Press, pp.139-58.

Hall, P. (1986), 'Racism and community education', *Forum,* Vol. 28, No. 2, Spring, pp.36-9.

Lawton, D. (1987), 'Cutting the curriculum cloth', *The Times Educational Supplement,* 1 May.

Lawton, D. and Chitty, C. (1987), 'Towards a national curriculum', *Forum,* Vol. 30, No. 1, Autumn.

Makins, V. (1987), 'The listening bank', *The Times Educational Supplement,* 12 June.

Moon, B. (1984), 'Challenging the deference curriculum', *Forum,* Vol. 26, No. 2 Spring, pp.35-8.

Mortimore, J., Mortimore, P. and Chitty, C. (1986), *Secondary School Examinations.* Bedford Way Paper 18, University of London Institute of Education.

Ranson, S. (1984), 'Towards a tertiary tripartism: new codes of social Control and the 17-plus', in P. Broadfoot (ed.), *Selection, Certification and Control: social issues in educational assessment.* Lewes: Falmer Press, pp.221-44.

Ranson, S., Taylor, B. and Brighouse, T. (1986), 'A Janus-headed revolution in education and training' in Ranson, Taylor and Brighouse (eds.), *The Revolution in Education and Training.* Harlow: Longman, pp.1-10

Reynolds, D., Sullivan, M. and Murgatroyd, S. (1987), *The Comprehensive Experiment: a comparison of the selective and non-selective system of school organization.* Lewes: Falmer Press.

Sexton, S. (1987), *Our Schools — a radical policy,* Institute of Economic Affairs Education Unit, March.

Simon, B. (1980), 'Education and the Right offensive', *Marxism Today,* February, pp.7-13.

_____ (1984), 'Breaking school rules', *Marxism Today,* September, pp.19-25.

Walker, G. (1984), 'Dream or nightmare?' *The Times Educational Supplement,* 27 January,.

Ysgol Emrys ap Iwan (1986), *Evaluation of a Modular Curriculum.* Ysgol Emrys ap Iwan/University of Lancaster.